A READING OF LIFE

A
Reading of Life

by

Sidney R. Lysaght

Essay Index Reprint Series

BOOKS FOR LIBRARIES PRESS
FREEPORT, NEW YORK

First Published 1936
Reprinted 1971

INTERNATIONAL STANDARD BOOK NUMBER:
0-8369-2060-0

LIBRARY OF CONGRESS CATALOG CARD NUMBER:
70-142659

PRINTED IN THE UNITED STATES OF AMERICA

CONTENTS

v

162892

I
FIRST OUTLOOKS

I

FIRST OUTLOOKS

IN THE BEGINNING GOD CREATED THE HEAVEN
AND THE EARTH.

What a simple, and easy and magnificent opening to the great story of Life!

That explanation of the Universe has long
ceased to satisfy the questioning spirit of man;
but, though the discoveries he has won from time
may have led him onward in the path of truth,
these are but measurable steps with the immeasurable beyond; and his baffled spirit may even
return to the haven of that first simple solution.

HE MADE THE STARS ALSO, says the old legend,
as if they were just a pleasant afterthought; but
it was the stars that first awakened in man a sense
of the immensity of the life in which he found
himself. Modern astronomy has revealed to us the
vastness of the material universe; it has shown us
vistas into space whose distances, measured in
light-years, no flight of the imagination can follow;
and it has compelled us to recognise the insig-

nificance of the Earth which is our home in the midst of this vastness.

It is remarkable that these immensities, though they may confound the intellect, do not humiliate or depress the human spirit. If it had been otherwise, if knowledge had revealed a universe whose paths were culs-de-sac, one which had limits beyond which neither life nor thought could pass, then these barriers would have appeared to us as prison walls. Though the infinite is beyond the comprehension of the mind, between the spirit and the illimitable there is a bond,—in our fearless outlook the assurance of a harmony between the spirit and the whole meaning of creation.

We are happy in the way in which the myriad worlds, sown in those awful profundities, are first presented to us. We see them through the nursery windows, or above the dark trees in the garden, or shining over still waters, and accept them as part of the scenery of our homeland. Even when we are older and have heard the bewildering tidings of astronomy, we look up into the heavens, not with dismay and fear of the unknown and alien, but with a tranquillity of spirit, an exaltation in contemplating a creation which has manifested itself to us in light and beauty.

The place of all others from which we can most clearly realise the vastness of the heavens and the boundaries of the Earth is the deck of a ship in mid-ocean. By day we can almost see the Earth's sphericity, almost feel the curvature of our course over the blue rings of the horizons; by night it is here only that we may behold the unbroken expanse of the celestial hemisphere. Fortunate are those who have been shown this wonder from the dark decks of a sailing-ship in southern seas, when the only sound is the wash of the waves under the bows, or the ship's bell striking the hour, or the call at the change of the watch, "Lights burning brightly. All's well!"—a call, an assurance, that would then seem to apply not only to the ship's lamps but to the stars themselves. Aloft we see the masts slowly swaying against those constellations that never before shone so clearly, or seemed so far away; and then the Earth itself becomes to us like a ship sailing through the unfathomable deeps of the skies. What a different vision of the universe is that of the dwellers in great cities, where the stars shine dimly above the streets or are extinguished in the vulgar glare of illuminated advertisements.

The most startling thing we realise in contemplating the universe is the fact that we live on an island world, separated by impassable deeps from every other world in that universe. Possibilities of signalled communication between one planet and another have suggested themselves, but that there is no pathway for man beyond the Earth's shores we accept as final. The dwellers on an island in the days before a ship ever put out to sea may have beheld over the horizon waters the mountains of a distant continent and dreamed of the new lands which their venturers might some day discover; but man looking out from his island Earth to the unknown spheres in that ocean of space which surrounds him, knows that no craft of his will ever reach the havens of those wonderlands.

There are tribes of uncivilised men who are unable to count beyond 5 and denote any excess over that number by the word *many*. Our measurements of the universe when they exceed a few million miles do not signify much more to us than the *many* of the savage. The nearest star outside the solar system is twenty-five millions of millions of miles away; but this is nothing compared with the distances of the Nebulae. From these, we are told, the light, travelling at the rate of eleven million miles a minute, would take from fifty to a hundred million years to reach us. From these tidings of the vast, of the unending succession of galaxies, of spheres of incalculable dimensions and unimaginable energies the mind recoils, the power of belief is staggered, and we almost envy the simpler point of view expressed in the words of the song,

> The little stars are brightly shining,
> Because they've nothing else to do.

We cannot imagine a universe which has no limits, nor can we imagine one which has no beyond: to our minds the finite and the infinite seem equally impossible. May it be that neither of these conceptions *is* a reality, and that the truth in which these contradictions are resolved must be sought along other pathways than those of the mathematician.

Is it, we ask, to miraculous accident or majestic design that we are indebted for our vision of the universe? If our planet had rotated, not from sunlight into shadow, but into the illumination of some other celestial body, or if it had been enveloped in a constant cloud canopy, these magic pathways through the heavens would never have been shown to us. Either we should

7

have seen nothing but the blue void of the day-light skies, or have speculated in vain as to what mysterious regions existed beyond the veil of the clouds. We have been shown those regions, but the Earth has tempered for us the shock of the vision by the veil of loveliness which her atmosphere has drawn across it. If we could be transported beyond that atmosphere, after sailing through the blue of the noon, or across the rose-red and opal archipelagoes of the sunset and twilight, the sun and the stars would appear to us as orbs of cold white light gleaming in skies of blackness. Is the provision, which has made the revelation to us so beneficent, accident or design? We have seen, we have not comprehended, but neither are we dismayed. On pathways of beauty fear is left behind. And looking into the depths of space we have felt that within our spirits are other pathways that reach beyond the stars.

The discovery of the Earth's boundaries, the realisation of its isolation, have changed man's outlook on life. Once he inhabited a world to which he conceived no limits. Over the uncharted seas lay the undiscovered: there was endless room for exploration and adventure. Now, except for a few tracts of tropical forest, or mountain pin-

nacles, or ice-bound waters of the Poles, no land
or sea remains unsearched. Once, gazing from our
western seaboards man dreamed of lands beyond
the islands of the Hesperides and at last he found
them. Now, looking from these same shores, he
knows that, instead of the Eldorado of his dreams,
he would find the roaring highways of New York
and the slaughter-houses of Chicago.

The old vision must have enlarged man's conception of his destiny. In a world with unlimited
room for discovery he must have felt the grandeur
of the scope for the progress of his race, and had
a dream of the future which enobled his present,
a promise of the distant which transfigured the
near.

But the old zest of the adventurer, the call to
the explorer, remains for man although the earth
no longer awaits his discovery; and though there
is no path for his feet beyond the confines of his
island world, his spirit accepts no boundaries.
Within his spirit he must still travel and seek
clues to the mystery of the creation of which he
is a part.

The awe which man feels in contemplation of
the universe of worlds beyond his reach and knowledge, is tempered by the very remoteness and

inaccessibility of that universe. The vastness
which a world such as our Earth would present
in relation to an ant-hill, a vastness from whose
crypts and transcendencies his paths were *not*
barred, might indeed have overawed him with a
realisation of his own insignificance and impotence. And is it not well that the roads beyond
our dwelling-place *are* barred to us? Do we not
gain more than we lose in the shelter of our
homely boundaries? Can we balance our loss and
gain? Here we are restricted, confined within our
island, whose population is already too large for
its well-being. Further increase in the numbers of
the human race points to devastating inroads of
the town into the country, to the complete obliter-
ation of the wild, to the desecration of the
beauty of Nature. The multiplication of man will
leave no room for the animals, except such of them
as may be preserved for his use. Already in such
densely populated countries as Japan the wild
birds have been destroyed, and in England there
are regions covering half the width of a county
where no field remains from which a sky-lark may
rise. A world of seas uncrossed and lands un-
mapped would have been in no such danger. The
streams of emigration would have flowed on un-

checked. The longing for adventure, the desire in man to discover and secure possession of a place of his own would have been fulfilled; and beyond his farthest penetration into the wilderness there would still have been freedom for the wild creatures of the forests and plains.

We can picture the exhilaration of the youth of our own day with such a prospect before them. How tame would seem the flight of those who now attempt to shorten by days or hours the time records connecting the hemispheres, or who face privation and death in planting their national flag on a plateau of Polar ice, compared with the magnificence of a winged adventure beyond the last outposts of the known world. There, in the room for expansion we can imagine the prospects that are denied to us in our inhabited globe. But may it not be well that we are forbidden the stupendous adventure, protected from the dark terrors of existence in a sphere whose boundaries we could never reach? From a birthplace beyond remote horizons, extinction might have come to man in the devastating incursions of its super insects, or under the unbearable civilisation of its demigods. Even if no such danger were to threaten us, in the vastness of this habitation we should have lost our home and would no longer have been brothers.

Boundaries make the home. To a child the boundaries are very narrow, extending no farther than to the garden gate or the field on which it opens, or perhaps to the top of the hill beyond; and the country over the hill is an unknown world. As we grow older the boundaries of the homeland expand until they reach the coasts of our native land, and our whole native country becomes home; and now that the confines of the earth have been reached and across its widest oceans we sail into friendly havens and are greeted with familiar speech, the Earth itself has taken friendly proportions. As countries separated from each other have developed nationality, so the insulation of the Earth among the spheres has produced a comradeship of its people which is moving towards the establishment of a terrestrial patriotism, an ambition to make our little planet worthy of a place in the galaxies of creation. And like a light in our darkness may shine the faith that our labours are not in vain, our achievements not doomed to oblivion; and that though the fabric of the earth may pass away, the spirit of its life, the song of its birds, the loveliness of its flowers, the deeds of its heroes, the inspirations of its master minds, the love of its faithful, shall remain and form a part of life's indestructible treasury.

✳   ✳   ✳

If we are fortunate in the way in which the stupendous spectacle of the universe is first presented to us, in aspects of beauty and light, we are no less happy in our introduction, along gentle steps of childhood, to the profound mysteries and incomprehensible decrees of life itself.

The first impression we receive on Earth is probably that of *home*,—of protection and sheltering boundaries, outside which are unknown wonderlands. We look round us with perpetual interest, almost with recognition, but without surprise. We wonder, but are not perplexed or mystified. We have not been launched on strange, wild, chartless oceans of Being; we do not arrive on the Earth as new-comers in foreign surroundings, dreaming of a past home and "that imperial palace whence we came". In the new world we are at home; and it is only after long years, when we have found this world too small, its gifts too fleeting to satisfy the desires of our hearts, that we dream of other spheres of life and imperial palaces beyond our present habitation.

In childhood, before we became conscious of ourselves, we were a part of all we saw: we were not separate creatures contemplating the scenes around us, we were incorporated into those scenes. Profoundly indifferent to the chemistry of earth and air, we were playmates of the wind, lovers of the wild-flowers, comrades of the creatures of wood and field. With dogs and horses we had real friendships; we put ourselves in their places, and often before going to sleep at night, listening to the winter wind, we were not in our own beds but in the stable with a horse or in the barn with a mouse; we entered into their lives before we realised our own. It was so with everything,— before we asked what life was, we *were* life; before the years began to close the gates of self about us, the whole comradeship of creation had entered into our hearts.

This is the first and instinctive happy reading of life, undarkened by the knowledge which afterwards tells of the struggle for existence, the cruelty or indifference of Nature, the oppression of the weak by the strong.

We cannot think of a beginning to our lives.

14

If we recall our earliest memories they do not seem like a beginning; they are more like an arrival to something expected, something of which we were already a part. It is as though the very fountain springs of being, which had no beginning, became conscious of themselves in our awakening.

So, not in any sudden revelation, but step by step, do we become aware of the astounding spectacle, the miraculous realities of life.

Stupendous as is the manifestation of the universe into which we are shown vistas from our Earth, but from which we are separated by impassable gulfs of space, we find around us other and no less marvellous regions of life from which we are not separated by distance, but only by our incapacity to comprehend them. The myriad activities of creation shown in innumerable forms of vegetable, insect, and animal life, hold secrets which lead us into wonderlands as magical as any we can dream of in the heavens.

If we could look upon our dwelling-place on the Earth for the first time with fully developed faculties, we should see its life like children, not in its intricate workings but as a whole. The picture, not the pigments, the results achieved, not the processes, would absorb us. Looking on almost any part of the Earth which has not been spoilt by man, should we not as new-comers exclaim, "On what lovely shores have we found ourselves!" The scene we looked on might be a meadow in our homeland in the early summer, a meadow bordered by woods in the freshness of their young green, with a river below it and hills in the distance beyond. The waving grass would be full of wild-flowers, the scent of the hawthorn and apple-blossom in the air, a lark singing in the blue.

No heaven we dreamed of could contain such loveliness, no triumph of creation excel the perfection of those forget-me-nots and marsh marigolds on the river bank, or invent a more exquisite fragrance than that of the meadow grass or the cowslips. That meadow-land in early summer gives perhaps an exceptionally happy first picture of our home on Earth; we might have chosen a forlorn moor,

Where the chill rain begins at shut of Eve
In dull November;

or a Siberian forest in a blizzard, or a Senegambian swamp; but the dark and dangerous places of the Earth are few compared with its sunlit havens and fruitful pasture-lands.

As new-comers, it would not only be the beauty of the scene, but the gladness also that would captivate us. Tidings of a joy at the heart of things would come to us in messages of colour and light and movement, in the song of birds and of water, "first of singers", in the laughter of children; and the common sights of farm and fold, the sheep scattered on the hillside, the cattle standing in the river shallows, the labourers at their fruitful toil would seem to tell of happy accord between the Earth and its creatures.

Not a sign of disillusion or tragedy, not a sign of cruelty, pain, or death. All these things would be hidden away. But while we are admiring the hawk poised on graceful wings above the meadow he is preparing to strike the field-mouse which his keen eyes have seen in the grass; in that exquisite gossamer a cunning little spider is waiting for its victim; those placid oxen are being fattened for the butcher; in the river the trout is devouring the salmon fry, and the angler is casting his line for the trout; and, passing on through that beautiful world, though we were greeted by the smiles of men and women, we should have to travel a long way before we discovered one who was contented, or on whose life the shadow of death had not fallen.

For the new-comer all these things would be as little in evidence as the machinery of the stage or the private cares of the clown are to a child taken to a pantomime; but he would realise them later when he found that he himself was not only a spectator but one of the actors.

It would seem then that the first instinctive attitude and response of man to his surroundings on Earth are expressed in admiration and grateful acceptance, in eagerness to enter into and become part of its activities,—and in a conception of life as a whole.

This is the child's outlook. With cruel but rare exceptions, his first impression of the earth is a happy one. Whatever disillusions may be in store for him, the first greeting of the Earth is a welcome, not a rebuff. He has found himself at home: the actual locality of the home matters less than you would expect: every place is attractive; what we afterwards describe as scenery counts for little: the ordinary natural presentment of life is sufficing. Let a number of people, gathered from different places, speak of their early associations, and there is hardly one who would not express love for his first home. It may be an English woodland

> Not wholly in the busy world, nor quite
> Beyond it;

it may be on the Atlantic seaboard of Ireland, where

> The fields slope southward abrupt and broken
> To the low last edge of the long lone land;

or on the cold north-east of Scotland beside "old grey stone cities imminent on the windy seaboard"; or among the canals in the flats of Holland; or on the Italian strands of the Mediterranean; or in snow-bound Canadian homesteads; or on the sunlit upland veldts of South Africa,— to each of these travellers his first home on Earth would be dear. Even for children prisoned in dull towns, whose first pictures of life do not even show a field, the divine alchemy of their spirits endows the railway embankment or muddy canal with enchantment or sets them dancing in an alley to the grinding of a gramophone as though it were the Pipes of Pan.

Is this first happy presentment of life a false one to be discarded subsequently by experience, or is there a clarity of vision in an outlook which is not dimmed by imperfect knowledge? Is it the dream of a creature who has not yet been confronted with the cruelty of Nature and of man, with the horror of pain and disease, with the awe of death,—or is it the true perception of a reality beyond our understanding, a reading born of an instinctive comprehension of life, an inspiration drawn from the very fountain springs of being?

Which is to be our guide to Truth,—that instinctive faith in life and in the eternal significance of our part in it, or the knowledge that throws doubt on such a faith?

One age may think it has found an answer and the next age may reject it; one man may find a beacon light where another sees but a will o' the wisp; but in our quest for truth, in our readings of life's hieroglyphs, it is inspiriting to remember that the first impressions we received were happy ones, that our first surroundings were beautiful, and that our first bonds were those of love.

II

A READING OF NATURE

II

A READING OF NATURE

YOUTH, unencumbered, unbewildered by the accumulation of knowledge and the conflicting opinions which that knowledge engenders, accepts life as a happy and splendid heritage. So do simple communities of unsophisticated men. The question, "Is life worth living?" never arises: even when the surroundings are unhappy it is felt that if the circumstances were altered all would be well. The young, the healthy, the untutored never question the value of life itself.

But this state of joy in our own vitality and our participation in the universal life is as unreasoning as the activities and obediences shown in what we call Nature,—in the plant absorbing the sunshine, in the bee seeking honey among the flowers, in the lark singing above the meadow. Man, that part of Nature which has become conscious of itself, on reaching maturity reflects on his knowledge and experience, and first of all he asks the question, "Is my life akin to that of the creatures of the wood and field and the air, which complete

23

their little parts and pass into oblivion; or have
I a destiny whose purpose extends beyond my
life on Earth?" For him, the answer to this question may decide the answer to the question, "Is
life worth living?"

Even the most fortunate, the very happiest
might ask this question if he believed that the
death of a loved one on whom his happiness de-
pended, was an eternal parting, or if he believed
that the work to which he had devoted his life
would have no permanent effect.

Imagination links man with permanent and
immortal things, and he distrusts his imagination: experience shows him the actual fact of
death, and he refuses to believe in death.

So his instinctive hopes and aspirations seem
to be in conflict with the lessons of his experience; but the instincts which make him rejoice
in his existence and put faith in his destiny are
the product of immeasurable time,—they are older
than the stars; and that knowledge which makes
him doubt the purpose and value of life is a birth
of yesterday.

The humblest man may feel a pride in his
ancestry: there is nothing *ready-made* about him.
The longest pedigree I have heard of is of one of

our Irish families in which there is a break, with
a note,—"About this time occurred the Deluge";
but that was quite a modern event: the pedigree
of every living person is equally long: to produce
that present individual there can have been no
break in the succession: the lineage is as old as
life itself.

And each of these individuals, equipped with
qualities won from the ages, endowed with ancestral memories, awakens on the Earth and finds
himself a separate being, embarked on a tremendous adventure,—an adventure great and inspiring
if he be a permanent conscious part of life's aim,
—great still, even if the adventure ends in the
tragedy of death.

The recognition of the amazing honour we have
received in becoming partakers of the heritage of
life comes to us so gradually through childhood
that we accept it as if it were inevitable. Perhaps
it is inevitable! But to most of us as we awaken
to consciousness of ourselves there comes a startling realisation of our situation—

> In the immeasurable lapse
> Of Time, amid the myriad haps
> Of Being, was it chance or plan
> That brought me hither and made me man;

That chose the hour and set me here:
Here in this land, in this abode,
This homeland on an island sphere
Beyond which man has found no road?
Why now, not then? Why I, not he?
Why here, not there?
And why at all, or if at all
Then why not always? What am I
Who call my life my own, yet die
And leave that life beyond recall?
Whose choice am I, for I chose not
The hour, the person, or the spot?
Oh, what inscrutable decree,
What law that had to be obeyed,
Fulfilled itself at last, and made
This, the inevitable ME? [1]

Whether man has been placed by design or has
arrived by accident, on Earth, he finds himself
in the position of an explorer in unknown regions.
And he naturally wonders why he should be confronted with mystery and uncertainty, why he has
no tidings of his destination. If he had definite
tidings his life would be very differently regu-
lated. If he had certain knowledge that it ended in
oblivion, he might well say, "Let us eat and drink
and get what fun we can out of it, for to-morrow we

[1] *The Immortal Jew.*

die". If he had assurance that he was a permanent part of the creation he sees, and that every action of his life had an eternal significance he would feel a pride in labouring for a cause which was worthy of self-sacrifice,—though even in this case I can imagine and even feel some sympathy with those who had their fling in life and didn't give a damn for the consequences. If man had any definite knowledge as to his destiny he would be in bondage to that knowledge. He has none, and he is free. He is an explorer, and though uncertain as to his fate, he is conscious of clues which may enlighten him. Ultimate truth may be beyond his reach, but he feels that he may travel on the road *towards* truth.

In his pursuit of truth, in his endeavour to solve the problems of existence, man appears to have but two pathways for his search: the investigation and study of the phenomena of Nature, and the examination of his own spirit.

When we speak of Nature we mean everything that exists apart from the intervention of man —everything, organic or inorganic,—winds and waters, mountains and rivers, pastures and forests, plants and animals. We separate from Nature the works of man,—from a wigwam to a cathedral, from a spade to a steam-engine, from an arrangement of fig leaves to a pair of trousers. These seem to have added a day's work to the original six of creation.

Man may be himself part of Nature, but we must regard him as distinct in this respect, that he is the only part of Nature which is conscious of itself and can look on the whole from outside, and the only part which is itself capable of conscious and deliberate design.

Man is a romantic and heroically minded creature, and would probably have preferred any miraculous or chivalrous interpretation of design in Nature to that of the slow processes and adaptations, the mean struggles and self-assertions through which science explains his evolution. The reasoned conclusions from observed phenomena have given him cold and dispiriting answers to the questions about those things which are nearest to his heart. He hesitates to accept these conclusions; philosophy and religion may tell him that they are not final; but no philosophy or faith which ignores them can have any substance, and in his search for truth his first steps must be along the path which science has cleared.

We should first therefore examine Nature judicially, uninfluenced by our own wishes, or the beauty or ugliness of the witness. We recognise without understanding the presence of a life-force. It manifests itself in countless material forms,—gaily, cruelly, irresponsibly, and yet in obedience to a necessity which we call law; expanding happily towards liberty of expression, shrinking fearfully from attack and destruction; in form fashioned for ravenous pursuit or for cunning escape from pursuit; in exquisite beauty, in loathsome ugliness. What a variety of forms! trees and flowers, insects, fishes, animals; a primrose, a butterfly, a humming-bird, a skylark, a tiger, a man; a fungus, a louse, a tapeworm, a shark, a weasel,—and all manifestations of the same life-force. Who dare call that life-force God? What conception could he have of a God, not only the source of power but the fountain of goodness and beauty, who could find expression in a mosquito, or a rat, or an Australian aboriginal?

We next observe that after this life-force has found expression in individual forms, the embodiments need sustenance, and find it in preying on each other. This is less marked in the vegetable than in the animal world, but even there we see a battle for space and the nutriment of the soil. The stronger dislodge the weaker, the pine forest replaces the grasses, the coarse weed chokes the delicate flower (until man comes to the rescue); and the jungle is a battlefield. And when we turn to the animal world we are appalled by the conditions under which it exists and the provisions for its sustenance. Hunter and hunted, victor and victim, spider and fly, singing bird and insect, hawk and singing bird, pike and minnow, weasel and rabbit! Man contemplates it with horror and yet he is himself the most predatory of all the animals. He devours the vegetable, the mollusc, the fish, the bird, the mammal. He robs the bee, he gelds the horse, and he celebrates his cruelties in thanksgiving to God:

> The fish in wave, the bird on wing
> God bade the waters bear,
> Each for our mortal bodies' food
> His gracious hands prepare—

a contemptible verse which I am sorry to say you will find in the Hymns of the Church of England.

"The most diabolical cruelties of man", says Dean Inge, "pale before the torments which Nature sometimes inflicts on her innocent victims."[1]

[1] Dr Inge in *Evening Standard*, Oct. 31, 1935.

There is no escape from the naked truth of the cruelty in Nature, and those who seek for God must look for Him elsewhere than in the designer of these conditions.

For sustenance the creatures evolved by the life-force prey upon each other: there is hostility between the species, often within it. For continuance a new force enters,—not hostility but attraction. Through separation, through difference, comes the consummation of union; through division, multiplication. Sex transfigures the universe. Its presence proclaims itself with jubilation, with pride and ostentation. In its manifestation the creature no longer hides itself from the observation of its enemies in protective colouring, but arrays itself in conspicuous and lovely raiment, or calls attention to its hiding-place in ecstatic song.

Death is always warning us to avoid it: life calling us to promote its continuance; or, rather, life (for death is mere negation) warns us against death, through pain and corruption, and attracts us to its service through beauty. From the fragrance or hue of a flower that attracts the insect for its fertilisation, to the grace of human form or the light in human eyes that attract man and

31

woman into matehood, beauty is the lure which
Nature displays to promote reproduction; or, might
we not say that it is the manifestation of that inspiration which directs life's higher evolution.

For beyond the provisions for survival and reproduction Nature reveals a progressive evolution
from lower to higher forms of life: and this
movement, the discovery of which was at first
regarded with hostility by those who were jealous
for the honour of creation, is, in reality, the one
reassuring thing in Nature,—the only foundation it gives us for a belief in a purpose that in-
spires its activities.

But whence comes this progressive movement
which has resulted on our Earth in the appearance
of man. If we assume that he and all the other
forms of life we see were evolved from a vital
material called protoplasm we are forced to conclude that this protoplasm was a seed in which
all the potentialities of the life we know were
hidden. The beauty of a rose is held in the insignificant grain of seed, but we know that this
would not be so if that seed had not fallen from
a rose. And if the spirit of man has been evolved
from protoplasm we must conclude that this
protoplasm was also a seed which had fallen from

a previous embodiment of life in which that spirit blossomed. Evolution then would seem to show us that the life which we contemplate on Earth had a parentage in some sphere of life beyond it.

But here again Nature points to no ultimate purpose,—only the exhibition on a gigantic scale in worlds, of what she has shown close around us in plant and animal; the seed, the flower, the fruit; and again the seed: no purpose beyond reproduction.

Nature gives suggestions, shows indications of a purpose in the activities of communities of insects, but denies it in the results achieved. These little worlds persist, but build no structure of life beyond their own; and the reading of Nature compels us to ask whether man is not, like the ant and the bee, fulfilling a destiny which has no object beyond its own temporary well-being and reproduction. Progress there may be, greater and happier human beings may be evolved, but there would be no permanent achievement,—for the Earth which brought them forth is itself, science tells us, doomed to extinction, and every hope and aim of man must perish with it, unless —and here science, if not positive in denial, is

33

dumb—unless there be communication through the spirit of man between the Earth, and homes of life beyond it. This possible path of the spirit is the only egress from our island world: through it, all that on earth has been accomplished might be retained and its seed become recreative; the labours and struggles of a million years might herald new advances and mark beginnings rather than ends; and everything that the Earth has brought forth of loveliness or nobility might be added to the treasury of universal life. In this direction the scientific study of Nature shows no light; but in our search for truth we shall find ourselves drawn irresistibly towards this, the only pathway that does not appear to be a cul-de-sac.

There are different ways of examining Nature. We may do this coldly, logically, as a lawyer examining or cross-examining a witness; or as a child questioning its mother. It is in such a filial relationship that the poets have read Nature, and this attitude alters the character of the enquiry,—threatening its impartiality but quickening its insight;—for the interpretation of Nature through the human spirit demands an examination of that spirit also.

The love of knowledge sends the man of science to the study of Nature: the love of Nature sends the poet to the study of her meanings. Science in the first place looks for information, poetry for beauty; and, taking different paths, they may meet on the borderland of discovery. Poetry sees the works of Nature in their wholeness; the poet may be also a botanist, the botanist a lover of poetry; but while the latter is primarily concerned with the structure of the flower, the former is conscious of some bond between its beauty and his own spirit and endeavours to interpret the meaning of that union.

Directly we approach Nature scientifically her deeper meanings elude us: directly we begin to analyse and anatomise, beauty is sacrificed. Water is one of the loveliest things in Nature, but we find no beauty in oxygen or hydrogen; and the noblest human form becomes hideous on the dissecting table. Especially does the human spirit defy the tests of scientific analysis, and the last place I should seek for knowledge of human nature would be in a text-book of psychology.

The great scientific minds have always ap-

proached Nature reverently. In her presence men
like Newton have been more conscious of their
own limitations than of the magnitude of their
discoveries; but the more general scientific attitude is one of self-satisfaction and an almost
Philistine dislike of imaginative readings of life.
The materialistic conclusions of the third quarter
of the nineteenth century darkened the outlook
of a past generation, as much as the fantastic
mathematical flights of recent years have bewildered our own. Science is always discovering
truths, but never the truth.

Nature when read in her wholeness,—read
naturally, that is as our own nature responds to
her, read with that truth and delight which, when
we are young and impressionable, almost all her
phenomena awake in us, a delight which no knowledge won from experience can destroy, will bring
us nearer to a knowledge of life than when cross-
questioned by a specialist for evidence, or put on
the rack by an inquisitor for confession.

The variety of embodiments and presentations
of the life-force is one of the first things that we
observe in Nature:

The world is so full of a number of things
That I'm sure we should all be as happy as kings,

said the child in Stevenson's verse; and though the burden of experience may lessen man's delight in the mere exhibition of life, the consciousness of its presence around him, of the unflagging zest, the infinite variety, gives his spirit perpetual sustenance. It would be easy to imagine a sphere in which Nature has shown no more variety than in an Arabian desert, or Arctic waste,—of a world in which there was only one type of vegetable life and one species of animal; but it would be difficult to imagine one in which more interesting forms and varieties of life or more beautiful expressions of it could be found than on our own island shores.

First, then, we should be thankful that we have been given such an interesting and lovely book of Nature to read. There may be pages we don't like, there are those who would bowdlerise this book and give us only the happier passages, but if we are seeking truth we must leave no page unturned.

More even than in the variety of its entertainments does Nature stimulate us by its activities. There is not a sign of stagnation; something is *going on* all the time. We find ourselves in a workshop of life where there are countless divisions of labour. We see that man's own chief activities are

similar to those of the whole animal world. Our
first work is for the provision of food to keep us
alive. The men who set out in the morning for
office or factory or farm land and return with
regularity every evening to their homes are following almost the same routine as the rooks who leave
their trees at dawn for their feeding-grounds and
return to their dwellings in the twilight. Both are
earning their daily bread,—or worms; both have
to choose mates and support families; both require
houses, though in providing this last necessity we
find a difference of procedure; the division of
labour has been carried farther with man than
with birds, and while the rook builds his own
house man very seldom does so, though it would
probably be a good thing for him if he had to.
In the main routine of daily life we act in much
the same way as birds and animals, and are thus
able to enter into fellowship with them. One part
of our being touches theirs; another part seems to
be remote from it. If man had no goal beyond the
fulfilment of his years on Earth, life could give
him little satisfaction beyond that which may be
felt by birds and animals; indeed I am sure that
if there were no further goal I would prefer to be
a rook, flying away in the morning with my com-

rades to my business in the fields, than a city clerk hurrying to catch a train on the underground railway.

Despite the survival of his predatory and hunting instincts, man undoubtedly has a feeling of goodwill for his other fellow creatures. In childhood the fellowship with bird and animal is almost equal to that for human beings: there is no natural antagonism, and the child learns with horror of their ill-treatment. It is *natural* for bird and beast, which are unreflective and unselfconscious, to hunt and prey upon each other, and it also appears natural for man, who is selfconscious and reflective, to regard himself as the friend of the animal creation, its protector, not its destroyer. But is this humane feeling natural? In the ordinary course of evolution should we not expect the predatory instincts to have increased, the strongest and most ruthless to have survived? May we believe that at the sources of life there are well-springs, not only of beauty, but of pity and fellowship, and that these emerge in Nature when it becomes self-conscious?

Our reading of Nature shows us the predatory instinct, the irresponsible cruelty: our reading of human nature shows that these proclivities exist

in man also, but that his ideals are in conflict
with them. How strong the elemental hunting
instinct, which originated in the necessity of providing food, remains in the human being may be
seen in the fascination of certain forms of sport.
The thrill which the angler feels when he has
hooked a salmon (and I suppose those patient
creatures who fish for perch or roach on canal
banks experience the same joy when their float
ducks); the satisfaction of the fowler who brings
down his bird, the stalker who kills his stag, have
little to do with the condition of the larder. Nor
are they just flattering tributes to the sportsman's
own skill, as, if so, a clay pigeon would do as well
as a snipe. They are survivals of the old hunting
instinct, and this is more conspicuous than anywhere else in fox-hunting, when the chase gives
nothing to the pot. Age after age man has become
increasingly humane to animals. To-day, in the case
of those slaughtered for his food, "humane killers"
have been introduced; but the very men who help
to promote this humanity forget it when they are
following hounds. I have been a supporter of fox-
hunting all my life, I recognise its exhilaration
and the fine qualities of courage and horsemanship
that it brings out, but nevertheless I can make no

attempt to defend it. Whether or not the fatten-
ing of beasts for the slaughter-house, the gelding
of horses and cattle, the taking away of calves
from their mothers, be justified as necessary in the
provision for man's actual needs, there is no justi-
fication for his "blood-sports"; and yet many of
us who feel this remain keen sportsmen. I emphasise this fact as showing how Nature and human
nature, the elemental instincts and the spirit of
justice and pity are commingled in our being; but
looking ahead, I feel sure that it will be in contests
with Nature which will test man's courage without
exercise of cruelty that he will prove his sports-
manship.

The history of man tells a long story of contention with Nature; but it is a friendly and
beneficent contention, and often this contention
seems to be composed in co-operation. The glory
and power of the ocean is never so fully realised
as when we see the waves thrown off from the
bows of a ship that is pursuing her own course.
Contention with the hardship of Northern winters
has bred the stoutest-hearted men the world has
seen, and under the directing hand of man Nature
has shown, among her loveliest aspects, the waving
cornfield and the sheltered garden.

Man is the part of Nature that has become self-conscious and responsible: if he is to be true to himself he must be true to Nature, and if he is to control Nature's activities he must control himself.

Bacon revealed a truth when he said that man conquers Nature by obeying her: it is equally true that Nature conquers man when he misuses her. To his confidence she responds with blessings, but to his tyranny with punishment. Man's ruthless mutilation of the face of the Earth for utilitarian ends has degraded his own dwelling-place; his undisciplined application of mechanical processes to his daily life has atrophied much of his own intelligent capacity. The immemorial relationship between man and Nature, the friendly contention and co-operation, the gradual adjustments, have been startlingly changed by the amazing activities of modern science. These suggest coercion rather than co-operation: they have condemned Nature to a subjection which amounts to tyranny, a scrutiny which is allied to vivisection. Man's intellectual power has outrun his moral sense, and the discoveries of science which have provided anodynes for pain and antidotes for disease have placed in his hands weapons of poisonous destruction. There is such a thing as a censorship in literature, and I would suggest that this should be extended to science, with greater penalties. If it would be too un-Christian to· condemn any chemist who produced a germ-poison or other material destructive to the human race, to be boiled in oil, which was the punishment of poisoners in the past, I would have him and every official of a government that proposed to make use of his invention for military purposes placed in a lethal chamber.

It seems clear that the scientific conquest of Nature can only lead to permanent progress when it is guided by moral and imaginative prevision, and has in view an ideal.

Approached sympathetically, man may rejoice even in the wild and rough and dangerous hostilities of Nature. His life is shaped by his contact with these forces, and he finds himself confronted not with tame trickles of life-forces, easy of control, but with the magnificence of immeasurable power;—energies which he can shape and re-create within himself into courage and service; sex-compulsion which he can transmute into fervent love; hardship which, in bearing, he can convert into strength. Man has been given the power

43   D

of using or misusing Nature. Externally to himself he can make or mar Nature, he can cultivate or destroy her beauty; but internally, within his own spirit that power of choice is far more momentous: within his own spirit he can shape the forces of Nature into Heaven or Hell.

It is difficult to-day to put ourselves in the place of those who lived in times before the discoveries of modern science. Even when we attempt to look beyond their revelations we are compelled to look *through* them; but we should be mindful that we do look through and beyond them and not merely *at* them. Our imaginative flights, unlike those of the Ancient World, have been given direction by special knowledge, but they should not be anchored to this knowledge.

Nature has always been the shaper of man's beliefs, however fantastically he may have read her meanings. He has been drawn to her, repelled from her; he has loved her, feared her, according to her aspects. He has conceived her anthropomorphically and peopled the unseen worlds with gods and demons and the visible world with

44

Naiads and Oriads, elves and fairies. Where he
has trusted there has been beauty in his beliefs,
as in his worship of Demeter and his recognition
of her gifts of fruitfulness; where he has distrusted
and feared there has been hideous superstition and
cruel sacrifice. I need hardly refer the reader to
the pages of *The Golden Bough* for illustrations.

With the development of the human intellect
the light of reason has freed him from most of his
superstitions, but has given little support to his
dreams of the unknown. But the dreams persist.
That quality of imagination which has often mis-
led him, when disciplined by reason remains the
pioneer on his path to the undiscovered regions
of truth. That imagination of the Old World
which pictured Naiads and goddesses, fauns and
fairies, is part of the creative conception of life;
something akin to it must have been present in
the vital force that produced man and woman.

No single book could give more than an outline
of the story of man's progressive reading of Nature
from the days of his first crude recognition of her
phenomena as powers outside his own being, to
our own days when he recognises in his own being
a self-conscious revelation of Nature herself. Here
I will not attempt even the briefest of summaries

of those stages and will speak only of the interpretation of Nature as she has been read in our
own age and in the minds of those whose imagination has been directed by scientific knowledge but
not imprisoned by it.

Our knowledge of Nature has been immensely
enlarged in modern times by patient scientific in-
vestigators like Darwin and Fabre, and sympathetic observers like Richard Jefferies and W. H.
Hudson. They have given us new insight into the
marvellous activities of creatures, in some ways
akin, in others immeasurably divided from ourselves. These observations are priceless, but it is
to the imaginative geniuses that we must look for
their interpretation.

There are two thinkers, both of them poets,
who seem to me to stand out among all others as
readers of Nature and interpreters of the relationship of the human spirit and Nature,—Wordsworth and Meredith. Meredith gives us the
modern presentation,—a rationalised, purgated,
ennobled presentation of an Old World's primitive belief in Nature as a Divinity, of Earth as
the mother. Meredith sees the Earth as a living
power and man as her chief expression:

46

On her great Venture, man,
Earth gazes while her fingers dint the breast
Which is his well of strength, his home of rest,
And fair to scan.

And throughout this poem, *Earth and Man*, is
shown the relationship of mother and child,—the
mother nourishing and training the child through
evolutionary periods, not only giving the sustenance and happiness, but also the trial of hardship
and danger for the strengthening of his spirit.
Even when, rebelling against his mortal fate, he
appeals beyond this mother to the unknown, it is
she who answers his cry:

If he aloft for aid
Imploring storms, her essence is the spur.
His cry to Heaven is a cry to her
He would evade—

and the poem ends,—

Meanwhile on him, her chief
Expression, her great word of life, looks she:
Twi-minded of him as the waxing tree
Or dated leaf.

Throughout all his Nature poems we are ex-
horted to trust in Nature in all her manifestations. Faith in her will bring the light of beauty

and goodness and gladness into our hearts, and
courage will show us that her terrors have no
reality.

> Nothing harms beneath the leaves
> More than waves a swimmer cleaves.
> Toss your heart up with the lark,
> Foot at peace with mouse and worm,
> Fair you fare;
> Only at a dread of dark
> Quaver, and they quit their form:
> Thousand eyeballs under hoods
>   Have you by the hair.
> Enter these enchanted woods
>   You who dare!

In *The Day of the Daughter of Hades* the poet
emphasises the exquisite delight to be found in
the common sights of terrestrial life. He is equally
insistent on the joy to be realised in a loving
acceptance of Nature's gifts, and the vital importance of the lessons which she gives us in trial and
hardship. In *Hard Weather* he tells us of the moods
in which Nature might also seem to be "her off-
springs' executioner", but continues:

> Look in the face of men who fare
> Lock-mouthed, a match in lungs and thews
> For this fierce Angel of the air,

A READING OF NATURE

To twist with him and take his bruise.
That is the face beloved of old
Of Earth, young mother of her brood.

.　　.　　.　　.　　.

Behold the life at ease; it drifts.
The sharpened life commands its course.
She winnows, winnows roughly; sifts
To dip her chosen in her source.

.　　.　　.　　.　　.

Earth yields the milk, but all her mind
Is vowed to thresh for stouter stock.
Her passion for old giant-kind,
That scaled the mount, uphurled the rock,
Devolves on those who read aright
Her meaning and devoutly serve;
Nor in her starlessness of night
Peruse her with the craven nerve:
But even as she from grass to corn,
To eagle high from grubbing mole,
Prove in strong brain her noblest born,
The station for the flight of soul.

Soul, kinship with eternal truth, is to be born
in us, not in looking for supernatural, but natural
inspiration; not in condemnation of Nature's
rough and cruel processes, or distrust of bodily
desires, but in embracing or contending with her
forces and re-creating them within ourselves.

49

Meredith's philosophy bids us have faith in the
appetites Nature implants in us, but exhorts us
to guide them. We are to see no enemy to the
"flight of soul" in the "kindly lusts", the warm
passions, but they must be met almost as we meet
hardship and danger: they must be ruled by the
spirit, not allowed to dominate it.

> Or shall we run with Artemis
> Or yield the breast to Aphrodite?
>   Both are mighty;
>   Both give bliss;
>   Each can torture if derided;
>   Each claims worship undivided,
>   In her wake would have us wallow.

> Youth must offer on bent knees
> Homage unto one or other;
>   Earth, the mother,
>   This decrees;
>   And unto the pallid Scyther
>   Either points us shun we either
>   Shun or too devoutly follow—

And his conclusion is that man's very efforts
to curb and regenerate the instincts of Nature in
his own spirit are inspired by Nature herself.
Earth thus is shown to be the source of all we are

or can be,—she the divine mother, and man the great venture she sends on into the unknown.

This philosophy is essentially opposed to the scientific materialism of Meredith's own time which read the development of life as the result of chance productions of opportunity during indefinite periods of time. It gives Earth the attribute of divinity and makes her the creative source of all we know. But if we are to accept Nature as the source of our inspiration, we then ask: Whence did Nature derive *her* inspiration; if Earth is the mother, whose child is she?—Meredith's philosophy makes no attempt to read farther.

To Wordsworth the inspiration comes from beyond the Earth.

> Earth fills her lap with pleasures of her own;
> Yearnings she hath in her own natural kind,
> And even with something of a mother's mind,
> And no unworthy aim,
>   The homely nurse doth all she can
> To make her Foster-child, her inmate man,
>   Forget the glories he hath known,
> And that imperial palace whence he came.

I cannot think that Wordsworth seriously believed that man has a celestial pedigree and is suffering a degradation in his life on Earth; but

51

rather that he is a new-comer, learning on Earth the responsibility of living, and receiving within his spirit an intimation of the divine source of the life he has come to share.

To Meredith if there be any imperial palace for man it is not something he has left, it is not behind him but beyond, to be sought by brave adventure along the pathways of experience, in acceptance or contention with the conditions in which Nature has placed him. There will be no imperial palace unless he himself build it.

Wordsworth gives us not so much a reading of Nature as of the human spirit in its relations to natural surroundings. Nature which to Meredith is the mother, is to Wordsworth the foster-mother: he conceives a presence external to Nature which finds expression through Nature and is in communion with the mind of man.

> And I have felt
> A presence that disturbs me with the joy
> Of elevated thoughts; a sense sublime
> Of something far more deeply interfused,
> Whose dwelling is the light of setting suns
> And the round ocean and the living air,
> And the blue sky and in the mind of man;
> A motion and a spirit that impels

All thinking things, all objects of all thought,
And rolls through all things.

The Earth is ennobled, humanity is uplifted by these readings of life; but in our search for truth we cannot shut our eyes to certain aspects of Nature which neither of the poets we are considering has referred to. If, as in Meredith's reading, Earth is the mother, giving us all our blessings, and even in her dark and stern moods chastening us for the production of responsibility and strength; if as in Wordsworth's reading, Nature is the expression of the divine spirit that "rolls through all things", what is to be said of her evil manifestations,—of the pain and desolation that result from her mad upheavals, her callousness, and the cruelty of her devouring instincts?

In the loveliness of flowers, the song of birds and of winds and waters, the light of setting suns, even in the blasts of winter, the rigours that test our endurance, we may recognise the loving mother, or the divine presence; but what of Nature's aspect in the tropical swamp where she is revealed to us in the alligator and mosquito,— what of her volcanic moods when with a shiver she destroys a town?

We cannot regard Nature as the ultimate source

of our inspiration. The evolution from the primeval slime to the discerning spirit of man demands
faith in an inspiration beyond our Earth, in a
purpose which transcends the irresponsible elemental forces, a purpose which is ordering them
and winning them to the service of great ends.

Man is part of Nature; he is of the essence of
the elemental forces, and he is also united with
the purpose beyond them,—"a compound of clay
and divinity" said Carlyle. He is the child of
Earth, but it is the light which has entered his
spirit from beyond it that makes him love her
beauty, read her lessons, and turn from her un-
purged crudities.

Science is the lamp which man has himself
kindled; it has built him light-houses on the dark
shores of the unknown: but his dreams, his quests
of truth lead him beyond the waters which his
little lamp of knowledge illumines; and if he
would venture on the farther ocean he must set
his course by a star.

III

BEAUTY AND TRUTH

III

BEAUTY AND TRUTH

No word, except perhaps *love*, has been given so
many meanings, uses, and misuses as the word
beauty. From a sunset to a beefsteak, from a human
countenance to the solution of a problem in
mathematics, the word is in constant request. I
propose now to confine it to its original meaning
as an impression on the senses, as it seems in all
other directions to be a misapplication. There is
a conception of the mind, drawn from physical
impressions, which is readily transferable to moral
or intellectual conceptions, and this has led to
such expressions as "a beautiful character", "a
beautiful solution", or even "a beautiful beefsteak". Really the word *beautiful* does not describe
personal character: it may be good or kind or
noble, and this kindness or nobility may express
itself in the lines of a countenance which may be
described as beautiful. When we call the solution
of a mathematical problem beautiful we are
merely using a physical term in illustration of an
abstract conception, just as we might use the word

57

hard or *tough* in speaking of the problem itself. And as to the beefsteak, from the point of view of the butcher or the cook, it may show signs of succulence which lift it high among its fellows, but in calling it beautiful they only mean that it is excellent. We may therefore leave the word beauty out of our consideration in its moral, intellectual, or utilitarian application.

In a later essay on Good and Evil I have defined the good as creative, evil as destructive; discerning in the good all that conserves, enlarges, and uplifts life, in evil all that degrades it. May we not define beauty as the manifestation through the senses of the essential goodness of life,—ugliness as the physical expression of evil.

Everything that we contemplate in Nature that we call beautiful is the expression or garment of life. The whole Earth is beautiful to us in its manifestations of life: the woods, the fields, and the flowers, the rivers that water the pastures, the mountains that gather the streams, the ocean from which the rain-clouds are fed and whose briny depths keep the whole earth sweet,—all are ministering to life and all are beautiful. If we survey the earth seeking for the absence of beauty we shall only find this in places where life has been destroyed or crippled,—in volcanic areas of ash and scoria, on desert plains where no rain falls, in the frozen plateaus of the arctic regions. Why, then, in speaking of places where life is abundant do we describe some as beautiful and others as without beauty? They are indeed all beautiful, but our faculty of comparison has led us to call only those things beautiful which are exceptionally so. A sort of datum line, a *stata forma*, is established, and everything above or below the standard has beauty accorded or denied to it. The most beautiful things are happily the commonest,—the light of day, the form and colour of foliage, the sound of wind and waters;—and because they are so common their beauty is seldom applauded unless it is magnified in some striking way,—where mountain height, or waterfall, or forest glade, presents form or colour or sound with unusual impressiveness. That there are degrees of beauty cannot be questioned: a flat monotonous country is less beautiful than one diversified with hills and rivers; but those lowland pastures with their exquisite flowers, their patches of furze, their hedges of hawthorn, their sedge-bordered ponds, are themselves so beautiful that no human imagination could have pictured anything to compare with them.

Beauty is the common physical manifestation of life, but where the life it expresses is placed in hostile or unharmonious surroundings the beauty will be dimmed or mutilated, where congenially placed it will be clarified.

The higher the level of life the more marked will be the beauty that reveals the vitality, or the ugliness that accompanies the degradation. If the most beautiful expression of life we have seen is in the human countenance, it is there also that we must look for the vilest, because in it are written, as nowhere else, the good and the evil.

Perhaps the simplest expression of beauty is found in colour. The light of life is dissolved for our vision into countless exponents of its beauty. The primary colours, blue, rose-red, yellow, are expressions of elemental beauty; but though the colours are themselves beautiful, the degree and quality of their beauty are dependent on the medium through which they are conveyed. It is the majesty of the stage that makes the crimson cloud at sunset more beautiful than the curtain in a room, that makes the same golden yellow a different thing when it is seen in a field of sunlit gorse or in an advertisement of mustard on a hoarding. Colour in a flower or on a humming-

bird's breast is more beautiful than in a tar-
product because of the exquisite texture of its
habitation.

And as to sound; most of the sounds in Nature
are beautiful: the voice of wind and water and
singing birds, the wild call of sea-fowl, the talk
of rooks, the lowing of cattle. Only when we
listen to the human voice do we hear the loveliest,
only then the most cacophonous of all utterances,
—because here again good and evil are assertive.

In considering the manifestation of beauty or
ugliness through sound, the belief I am uphold-
ing that beauty has a foundation in the essential
goodness of life is supported by the fact that
harmonious sounds are beneficial and discordant
ones injurious to the auditory sense,—the most
unpleasant sounds we know, such as the filing of
a saw, the scream of railway whistles, the jar of
musical instruments out of tune, being definitely
harmful to the human nerves. And if we turn to
the sounds produced by animals and men, though
they may not so directly affect the nervous system
they enter the spirit and tell of a deeper good
and evil. In the songs of birds, in the voices and
laughter of children, in musical harmonies, the
beauty of life is proclaimed: in the howlings of

an imprisoned dog, the shriek of a woman, the yell of a lunatic, we are shown the fear and pain and despair that lurk under the shadow of death.

Apart from their associations, the mere physical sounds of rippling waters, of wind in the trees, of singing birds, and the purer tones of the human voice, are beautiful in themselves; the screech of metallic friction, the snore of uneasy sleepers, the snarl of an angry dog, are ugly sounds; but the essence of their nature, their origin, contributes largely to the effect. We recognise pure beauty of sound in the song of a skylark or nightingale, but in listening to it the scene of presentation affects our appreciation. Listen to the note of the nightingale conveyed through a wireless transmitter to a street in London,—though we hear the notes and admit the beauty, how much less lovely they sound than when we heard them breaking the silence of the moonlit woodland. And will not a still deeper beauty be added to that music by a memory of the lines about

> Magic casements opening on the foam
> Of perilous seas in faerylands forlorn,

which told of the dreams of the human spirit which that bird's song created?

A more complex expression of beauty or ugliness in sound is heard in the articulation of human speech. Between the low sweet tones of one woman's voice and the scraping thinness of another's there is all the difference between music and noise. And it is almost the same with the speech of nations. Listen to the talking of Tyrolese mountaineers and you will hear something like song, and to that of a group of Hindus and you will be reminded of the chattering of monkeys. In the speech of the peasants of the Scottish Highlands and of the south of Ireland there is a rhythm and a significance of intonation; in that of the educated Englishman an expressionless conventionality, in that of the American an aggressive and monotonous emphasis. Listen to the speaking of young children and you will notice its scale, its intensity of tones,—tones which express their feelings of interest, gaiety, or distress,—listen to their laughter which is the very voice of innocent happiness! With children, and with some simple peasant people, their speech expresses the *truth* of their emotions, and it has beauty: in the conventional tonelessness acquired by their elders there is no expression of their feelings and there is no beauty.

63

It is beyond my present purpose to enquire into the causes which have given a beautiful speech to one people and an ugly one to another; we see that it is so, and can only regret that a language like Greek, at once so beautiful and so vigorous, should have been allowed to decay, that the melodious cadences we hear in the speech of our European peasantries should be doomed to extinction with the advance of cosmopolitan intercourse, and that such ungraceful speech sounds as the American and Cockney should be spreading through the world. Both of these are ugly, and both are untrue, or only express a partial truth.

That beauty and ugliness are expressions of good and evil is even more apparent in the sense of smell. By this sense we are attracted to the healthful and guarded against the poisonous. The smell of the earth after rain, of flowers and fruit and grass and corn are all beautiful and all tell of life: the smell of corruption, of drains and tropical swamps, of unclean humanity or monkeys are ugly, and all tell of danger or degradation of life. The scent of primroses or hawthorn in the air is a manifestation of the pure beauty of life: the odour of an abattoir of its disgrace.

In considering taste (in its application to food),

64

the word beauty has less significance than in the
case of the other senses. We may apply it without
hesitation to most fruits, to some vegetables and
cereals, to tea and coffee and wine; but when we
take a wider range we may doubt its admissibility.
High game or strong cheese may be agreeable to
an acquired taste in man, as putrescent carcases
may be attractive to rats or vultures, but we can
hardly call these tastes beautiful. I think that
taste can be allowed to apply the epithet beautiful
to that which has the approval of the sense of
smell, and that here also kinship between the ugly
and decadent is descernible.

I am not quite clear as to what Keats meant
when he said "Beauty is truth, truth beauty".
Did he mean that beauty is an expression of truth
through the senses, and truth an expression of
beauty through the intellect? I have been trying
to prove the connection between the beautiful and
the good, but truth and goodness are not one.
Truth is a revelation of what *is*, and though its
revealing may be good, the thing revealed may be
bad and not beautiful. Perhaps the real meaning
of that line is that beauty cannot exist unless it be
founded on truth. To take an illustration: friends
of mine, travelling in Japan in the blossoming

season, arrived at a country inn after nightfall, and from their bedroom windows saw a magnificent picture of cherry-blossom in the moonlight, and were enthusiastic in admiration. In the morning this proved to be the hotel washing spread out on bushes. Of course if they had known this at the time, though the appearance would have been the same, they could have felt little admiration. Beauty exists not only in the effect but in the knowledge of what produces the effect. No imaginative simulation of cherry-blossom could give the beauty of the real thing. And as another illustration: I knew a guest at a hotel who was kept awake the first night he was there by the irritating sound of what he believed to be a steampipe in the heating apparatus. Next night, after discovering that this was a mistake and that the sound came from the water of a stream running over a weir close by, the noise which had kept him awake became a music that lulled him to sleep. In each case the truth became an essential part of the impression. In the former it made the semblance of beauty futile; in the latter its revelation of a lovely origin endowed a monotonous sound with charm.

But a question arises here that must be considered. As to the laundry in the moonlight it may be argued that no subsequent discovery of the truth about it could undo the sensation of beauty experienced under the misapprehension, and that for the occasion, therefore, the beauty was not founded on truth, but was a picture in the observer's mind. To this I would agree with the reservation that the observer's vision of beauty in the illusion was ultimately traceable to truth. He had a stored value for flowers in moonlight drawn from previous experience of their reality. If the truth has not been in his mind he would not have admired the counterfeit. And as to the weir and the steampipe,—assuming their sounds to be identical, I can only suggest that this sound was not in itself either beautiful or discordant, and that its only value was in the message it conveyed. Certain words are neither beautiful nor ugly, but convey beauty by their meaning. Neither could the laundry remain beautiful nor the waterfall irritating after discovery of what they really were, and I maintain that there is no permanent beauty that has not a foundation in truth.

It is doubtful if an instance can be cited of beauty unallied with truth. In the human countenance the man's is allowed to speak for itself, but the woman's is not unfrequently subjected to falsification, and paint, powder, and acquired hair may produce a simulation of beauty. But could anyone maintain that knowledge of the artificiality of a woman's complexion would not make her less beautiful. The deception, when Nature is closely imitated, may be effective, until it is discovered: when it departs from Nature and no longer deceives, the untruth produces positive ugliness, as in the Noah's Ark vermillion which some young women of these times put on their lips, or the mean precision of their plucked eyebrows. An artificial flower may deceive the eye at a little distance, but it will lose its beauty when we discover that it is made of paper. Stage carpentry, the lath and plaster palaces of a White City, may show us amazing scenes; but though we may admire the skill of the construction there is no enchantment of beauty in the illusion.

From its simplest to its most complex presentments beauty is *real*. It is interwoven with truth and knowledge. It is possible that the beauty of colouring may be more marked in the reds and golds of the Autumn woodland than in the young greens and madders of the Spring; but in the Spring scene there are tributaries of beauty which are lacking in that of the Autumn. We know in the Autumn that the colour is produced by decay (but as that decay is the herald of "the coming to-be" it is good and its expression is beautiful), we know that the ground beneath the trees is damp and cold, and that no birds are singing overhead. In the Spring everything speaks of young life; the grass is full of flowers and pleasant to lie on and the air is full of song. All these things enter into our contemplation of the scene, and though the splendours of November may provide finer subjects for a painter than the freshness of May, most of us will find more beauty in the vernal scene than the autumnal, because it gives us not only the colour of the woods, but the song of the lark and the smell of the white thorn.

You may see in such places as South Wales a beautiful valley, but when you know that you have but to climb the hill which bounds it to look on another scene defaced by collieries and smelting furnaces, the beauty of the valley is injured: you cannot isolate it from its surroundings. I would go farther and suggest that a knowledge of the people who live in a place affects its beauty. If in the upland pastures of a mountain country those little farms and cottages inhabited

by a simple peasantry were replaced by the shoot-
ing-lodges of the rich or the hotels of the tourist,
much of the enchantment of the scene in which
the people had an immemorial place would have
passed away: the old glamour and the physical
beauty are interwoven.

It is clear that what we call beauty would have
no meaning apart from the mind that perceives it.
If there were no beings endowed with senses, a
world might produce the same trees and flowers,
hills and streams; and though the form, smell,
and colour of these might be, as we believe, the
garment and expression of life, the word beauty
could not be applicable, if there were no minds
on which impressions could be made.

Beauty, as Wordsworth said, is born of the
union between the natural aspects of life and the
discerning intellect of man, which, of course, is
a very different thing from the assertion that it is
essentially a subjective vision. The latter view has,
however, been strongly supported and requires
examination. Why, it is asked, should there be
difference of taste in beauty,—difference resulting
at times in the same object appearing beautiful
to one and ugly to another? A Chinese woman
may be beautiful to a Chinaman and ugly to a

European; the furniture and architecture of the Victorian period were considered beautiful in the nineteenth century and ugly in the twentieth; sweet champagne is pleasant to one palate and nauseating to another; a symphony of Beethoven is a jumble of vibrating sounds to a man whose heart may be melted by the sickly sentiment of a negro melody; the verses of Mrs Ella Wilcox or Mr T. S. Eliot may have actual beauty for readers who would find none in Milton or Browning. How, then, can there be any standard of beauty? they ask. Is it not all a matter of individual taste?

The instances just given are of the more complex manifestations of beauty. We have already discussed its simpler forms and seen in them the natural raiment of life. Here there was little difficulty in showing that beauty is not a matter of individual taste, but has a universal appeal. No one outside a lunatic asylum will question the beauty of a rose or a sunset: failure of appreciation would show defect in the receiving instrument; but when we consider beauty in its more involved manifestations it is not so easy to be definite. Is the beauty of wine, of the human voice and the human countenance, of poetry, of architecture, a matter of individual judgment? Let us take the case of wine,—not an easy one to decide, for it is complicated by the introduction of alcohol, and a connoisseur of port may read into its flavour the anticipatory glow in his stomach which would be absent in his verdict on raspberry-vinegar. I can only argue that education, the opportunity of testing a number of different growths or seasons and choosing between them will almost invariably lead to a selection which establishes a standard. Round this standard there may be minor variations or preferences, but the fact that *knowledge* leads to a general agreement in judgment is an indication that there is a foundation of truth in that judgment.

Even more complex is the reading of a woman's beauty; for as alcohol enters into the appreciation of wine, sex plays its part in our admiration of women. Sex, indeed, is so near the source of life that it is near the source of beauty; and I would suggest that, as all sound old wine has some beauty, so have all sound young women. But how shall we set up any criterion? The Chinese woman attracts her countryman and has no charm for the European; a blonde pleases the taste of one man, a brunette another's; plumpness or slimness of form, serenity or vivacity of expression, each has its admirers, but while admitting that there may be beauty in all I maintain that there is nevertheless a basis of judgment. I must return to my definition of beauty as the manifestation through the senses of the goodness of life. This is shown in the human being in various forms,—in a bodily frame which is active and strong, in a face which has the colour of health, in features that indicate vitality. It is shown also in the expression which tells of kindness of heart or brightness of intellect, or in sex attractiveness. The result is beauty in degrees varying with these exhibitions of life's goodness. Conversely, a deformed body, a colourless skin, a narrowed forehead and receding chin, a cruel mouth and a dull eye, tell of defective vitality or an evil spirit, and produce ugliness. The best and the worst embodiments of life are found in the human being, and in the human countenance beauty and ugliness reach their extremes.

But though we may have succeeded in showing that there must be a foundation for beauty in goodness and truth, it must of course be admitted that there are degrees in its expression and wide scope for individual preferences. The characteristics of the scenery in which we were bred, and

the types of countenance of our fellow countrymen make a special appeal to us. The mountaineer
may fail to see the beauty which the Dutchman
finds in his canal-banks, but the beauty is there.
They would be agreed in finding no beauty in the
East End of London or the Kalahari desert. The
European and the Chinaman read beauty in different types, but their reading of beauty is based
on the same foundation. For both of them, expression of the goodness and joy of life, of health,
intelligence, warm-heartedness, will be written in
the countenances in which they see beauty, the
opposite characteristics in those in which they
find none.

The quality of the surroundings, the interest,
variety, and responsibility of occupation make
their mark on the countenance. Rugged and rough
though it may be, there is a certain beauty of the
elements in the faces of hunters and fishermen,
sailors and shepherds, which is generally absent in
those of city clerks, waiters, bookmakers, shop-
walkers, and town councillors. Modern competi-
tive trade, with its need for astuteness, self-
advertisement, push, on the part of its regulators,
—mechanical, monotonous, specialised labour in
the case of its workpeople,—has produced a type

of countenance which, when not ugly, is without interest or beauty. The deterioration in physical attraction produced by sedentary or mechanical occupation is less evident in women than in men. Hardship, danger, adventure, bring strength to a man's form and features, but comfort and security are more congenial to the happy development of women. Still, where there is deterioration in the man, the daughters' appearance will suffer for it, and on the masses of our town-bred women the artificial conditions are making their mark, and regulating such charm as youth and sex give them to a monotony of type. The beauty of natural surroundings, "the beauty born of murmuring sound" no longer passes into their faces, and the emotions aroused by the sentimental romance of the Cinema can hardly be considered a substitute.

It is difficult to compare the beauty of animate and inanimate objects,—of a sunset with a human countenance. The individual spirit which is the highest exponent of life known to us, expresses itself physically in the highest form of beauty. A lovely scene: a lovely face! We use the same word for both and yet how great a difference there is. In the beautiful face of a woman, the passionate longings, the tenderness, the joy, all that we most desire in life itself, is shown to us; it holds and reveals to us our dreams in physical reality. And yet we can hardly call it physical, so immaterial is the manifestation: after taking into full consideration the quality of human eyes, their setting, their colour, what material explanation can be found for the love-light that sometimes transfigures them?

The relationship of beauty to truth in art, though more complicated than its other relations, is, I believe, not less real. Art is man's contribution to creation,—"all other work is only discovery, or manipulation of what is already created, but in art a new thing is born. The divine within man touches the clay or the string, or the word, and we are shown a beauty that was not here before."[1] It is a great claim to make for man that he should have contributed to the creation. If he had no part in his own creation (which is by no means certain, and is a question discussed elsewhere in this book), then he may deserve no more credit for his contributions to it in Art than for his procreation of children, except that the former does demand more labour, more sacrifice. Whatever his personal contributions, they are essen-

[1] *My Tower in Desmond.*

tially the result of what we call inspiration and are born of the alliance of his spirit with a spirit beyond himself,—the eternal creative spirit which we may call divine. The starting point of all our beliefs,—that life is good,—must be followed by the belief that creative art, which adds to life, is good; and I would go farther and say that all art which is creative is beautiful. Here, then, is a test for a work of art: is it creative, or destructive —is it an addition to, an illumination of life, or a disfigurement and adulteration?

A great deal of artistic work which is creditable but imitative is being produced, and also a great deal which is spurious. To speak of literature, the verse writers who deserve like schoolboys to be set impositions for their false quantities and bad syntax, or thrashed for their effeminacy, and the writers of fiction whose attitude to life suggests that their inspirations are almost entirely abdominal, are hailed week by week in the press as geniuses. In every generation a few, and only a few great works of art are produced and survive, and it will be found that these have their roots in truth and health, and that they are beautiful. The poetic exercises which express the superficial sentimentalities or the cynicisms of a period are evanescent. Even the greater producers of the unreal can have little permanent influence. Though we admire Byron's wit we see that his poetry was based on false emotions, on a misreading of life and of his own spirit, and it has not survived. Though we cannot admire Wordsworth's wit, and though his verses are often crude we feel that his poetry has its inspiration in truth, and on occasions this inspiration finds expression in a beauty which remains a joy for ever. For the artist, the poet, to be capable of seeing life truly he must be capable of reading his own spirit: the truth must be also within himself.

So in painting: there must be truth to Nature, fidelity in delineation. No imaginative gifts will enable an artist whose drawing is bad and whose colouring is untrue to paint a great landscape or portrait. Schools or cults of painting and sculpture, in revolt against stereotyped or anaemic expressions of the beautiful, have gone to the extremes of grotesqueness and ugliness. We have seen haystacks painted pink, buildings drawn out of the perpendicular, women with rectangular bosoms. We have seen the poet's dream of a Madonna embodied by sculpture in the figure of a negress. The reactions against conventions,

78

against "prettiness" have their use and lesson; but in the works they produce their ugliness proclaims their untruth, and their untruth condemns them to extinction.

In architecture, too, truth is a fundamental basis of beauty. The massive foundations, the strength of the structure are essential to our delight in contemplating the soaring spire. You may see in the streets of London more than one pile of magnificent shop-fronts, in which the range of columns which should be on the ground as a support to the superstructure, is on the first storey; and, though there is a concealed iron framework, these columns actually appear to rest on the glass of the shop windows. Whatever beauty the building might have had is damaged to the mind by the false appearance in structure.

The healthy mind of average capacity has a pretty true instinct in recognition of good and evil, and also of beauty and ugliness, but may be incapable of appreciating the depths and refinements of beauty which are revealed to the more sensitive artistic temperament. The former may be limited in its scope but it never goes far wrong: it never mistakes ugliness for beauty; the latter when not united with a sane intellectual outlook produces the schools and cults of eccentricity and decadence in literature and art which arise in every generation. There are periods in which false standards have been so dominant that in after-times it has been imagined that they had general approval. My view is that in every generation of false gods there was a *corps d'élite* of the best minds who protested against them,—for instance that all we call dull and absurd in Victorian fashions of art and literature was at the time objectionable to the discriminating,—and though our present period may be laughed at in the future for its impudent attempts to glorify the ugly, it is already being laughed at by the wise. In short, a permanent standard of beauty remains through the ages, though there are periods during which false standards become popular. True prophets arise to put the false ones to shame, and between the true prophets there is a kinship: they speak with different tongues, and from different points of vision, but in their many voices there is harmony, whereas the false prophets are in perpetual disagreement, for they have no common faith.

The saying that "great wits to madness are allied" is untrue. If we consider the greatest geniuses of the world we shall find that they were essentially sane, perhaps the sanest and most clear-seeing of all men. It is not among great geniuses that we shall find indications of madness, but among those in whom the artistic faculty is pronounced but not united with intellectual balance, who have a gift of expression but no true reading of life to express. To speak only of English literature, in the category of those whom we recognise as essentially sane we shall be able to place almost every great writer in verse or prose,—Chaucer, Spenser, Shakespeare, Milton, Pope, Fielding, Scott, Wordsworth, Tennyson, Browning, Dickens, Thackeray, Meredith, Hardy—to name no others; in that of those allied to madness we can hardly place one, unless, indeed, Blake be an exception; but though his genius is conspicuous, and though he has disciples who admire the incoherence and nonsense in his work more than the beauty, how much greater he would have been if his vision had not been often obscured. The past gives us no great names in support of creative alliance between genius and madness: those in whom this discordance with healthy life existed have not survived; and if we must therefore ask for instances from recent times, and such names as Oscar Wilde, D. H. Lawrence, or James Joyce, are given in evidence, we can only wonder at the success of the imposture, and recognise the appeal of the decadent to the hypersensitive neurotic mind.

It is an inspiring reflection that all the simple and common manifestations of life are beautiful; sunshine and fresh air, fields and flowers, rivers and mountains, the sound of wind and waters. It is a glorious thing that colour, the child of light, which is the revealer of life, is beautiful. Or will it be objected that this appreciation is no more than an adaptation of our perceptions to their environment,—that we only call these things beautiful because they are congenial to the senses they evoked? I am quite content, for this would also support the view I set out to establish,—that beauty is the expression of the essential goodness in life, and that in its response to beauty the human spirit has found the pathways of truth.

IV

LOVE AND SEX

IV

LOVE AND SEX

THERE is no word except *beauty* that has been given more meanings than the word *love*, even when speaking of human relationships. I shall now consider it chiefly in the bond between man and woman.

Whatever may be the ultimate goal of life, there can be no doubt as to a purpose in its provision for continuance, through reproduction, of its creatures; and though this might have been possible without the incentive of sex attraction we can imagine nothing else that could have been so irresistible, or, in its happiest expression, so beautiful; indeed it seems so supreme an achievement of creation that we are almost compelled to believe that it is a reality which is universal and not merely a phenomenon of our island world.

And yet? May not our subjection to this power incapacitate our judgment; may we not, indeed, be wrong in assuming that the love between man and woman is the most interesting and absorbing thing in life, and that a world without it would have lacked romance? Might it not be considered that it is a tyrannous and distracting emotion, a mere compulsion to satisfy a desire, comparable to hunger or thirst; and that if this need, this affinity, had been absent, the whole tenor of life would have been saner and its activities freed for the enjoyment of a higher happiness?

In support of such a contention we might be asked to look at life as it appeared to us in childhood before these "troublesome desires" were awakened. It was a period of intense interest in everything, of magnificent capacity for enjoyment. Every bodily activity,—running, swimming, manual labour,—was a pleasure; everything in Nature,—flowers and birds and animals,—attracted us; we entered sympathetically into the lives of dogs and horses and human beings, — except, perhaps, girls; — there was romance in all farming and structural work, and an eagerness for knowledge that did not come out of school books. There was no sex in our loving: our devotions were for elder brothers who were good cricketers, and jolly seniors who treated us as friends. We were part of all life until sex concentrated the attention on self. Might we not picture a sphere in which the attraction between

86

the sexes was absent, where such interests and joys as we knew in childhood were continued and increased; where all that was adventurous and romantic to us in those early days might have found fuller expression through matured faculties, and have given a greater emancipation of spirit and a truer foundation of happiness?

Persons for whom the sex attraction hardly exists would no doubt take this view. I knew a distinguished professor of mathematics who described his own "coefficient of nuptiality" as small, and who once said that while he recognised the fact that men as a rule did need the sex relationship, he, personally, found that a good run round Hampstead Heath (where he resided), and a rub down afterwards, was a perfectly satisfying substitute.

The philosopher may find an intellectual, and the mystic an ecstatic serenity; and both may be able to seclude their lives from the dominating influence of sex attraction; but are they not also separating their lives from life itself? Is there not a secret, a meaning in life missed by them and revealed to every pair of true lovers?

There is a story of a lecture delivered by a lady on the rights of woman, which she concluded with the words, "We only ask to be treated as the equals of men—surely we are as intelligent; and, if there be a physical difference between men and women, after all how little is that difference!"— whereupon a navvy in the audience rose to his feet and solemnly exclaimed, "Three cheers for the little difference!" That little difference has given life its chief interest: the joys and tragedies it has created, the admiration it has evoked, the degradation it has inflicted, the devotion it has inspired, have provided the most absorbing part of the story of humanity.

So tremendous an influence is this force of sex attraction in human life that it is not surprising to find that it has become at one time an object of worship, with temples and deities, and at another has been viewed with distrust and surrounded with restrictions and penalties.

> Or shall we run with Artemis
> Or yield the breast to Aphrodite?

asks the poet; and he proceeds to show disaster ahead if we shun, or too devoutly follow either. Enforced celibacy, "sex starvation", as it is now called, may be as injurious to the individual as incontinence; but, to the Race, periods of licence are far more dangerous than periods of narrow puritanism; for the natural appetites are in no danger of permanent suppression, and a course of abstemious dieting may even be invigorating. Defining good and evil as that which is protective of life and that which is destructive, we see that the tendency of licence is to check fecundity and of continence to increase it. Among simple and religious peoples, where the standard of sex morality is high, there are large families, in sophisticated communities, where the standard is low, and the sex relationship has been specialised and separated from its natural purpose, the birth-rate is small; and promiscuity inevitably leads to sterility. I cannot doubt that the maidens who were

> Strait-laced, but all too full in bud
> For puritanic stays,

made good sweethearts and better wives than the young women who carry contraceptives in their dressing-cases.

The distrust of the natural instincts, the mortification of the flesh, the religious fanaticism which regards the sex relationship as something actually evil (which in cases such as that of Origen even led to self-mutilation, and in Tolstoi's to feelings

of contemptuous revulsion), may all be regarded
as a lack of sanity in minds obsessed by their
recognition of the tyranny which this force, when
unbridled, exercises upon humanity. We may
dismiss their views, together with those of the
mere hedonist, from our reading of life. The
elemental forces of Nature, when, as in the sex
attraction, they are allied with the human spirit,
need control, but we must not distrust them: we
must make their strength ours. That privilege of
control and guidance of these forces is the greatest
responsibility that man has been given.

Whether we are satisfied to accept a purely
physical explanation of sex difference as a phase
of evolution, or hold that it is an elemental reality,
an inevitable expression of the universal life
spirit, we recognise that its existence in the human
creature has done more than anything else to make
life stimulating. It gives one half of humanity a
perpetual interest in the other half. The humblest
has inherited its endowment in as full a degree as
the highest, and for no wealth would the poorest
exchange its potentialities. It opens the gates for
all to the realms of wonderland, and even in
the dullest surroundings points to paths of adventure. The adventures may be ignoble or splendid,

they may vary from those of the poacher or buc-
caneer to those of the knight-errant; but the difference of sex, the presence of "one of those other
strange creatures", makes romance perennial.
Through it man and maid feel the thrill of the
moving impulses of life in their own conscious
being, and hear whispers of a mystery that is older
than the stars.

The predominant interest which sex relations
give to life is reflected in literature. Nearly all the
world's great stories are those of love, and in the
minor stories also, where the theme has not been
love, it has been gallantry. In the fusion of the
sex passion with love the human spirit has created
an ideal,—one not often fully realised but nevertheless attainable. Disappointments, disillusions
are only too frequent, but the inspiration remains. There is a deep desire at the bottom of
man's heart that true love should triumph, and
in spite of every cynical experience, the audience
at a play, the reader of a romance, welcomes a
happy ending. It is an interest which has increased as civilisation has advanced and human
nature became more complex. In the earlier romances the love interest was secondary to the glori-
fication of heroic deeds, and though Helen was

the cause of the Trojan war, the *Iliad* had no need
of her for its success; and in the *Odyssey* how small
a part of its romance is found in love or amorous
adventure! A distinguished modern author recently
told us her impression on reading the *Odyssey* for
the first time. "Why", she asks, "is there so little
about sex in it? After a course of the best modern
authors the thing seemed positively as if it must
have been bowdlerised." The amazement of a
modern lady that any great romance could have
been possible without the sex interest shows how
dominant that interest has become, and how
much more important woman is now than then.

In the past the presentation of sex relations in
the guise of true love was simpler and happier
than it is to-day; in the guise of gallantry it was
perhaps grosser, but less insidious. Heroic qualities in the man, innocence and trust in the maiden,
are found in most of the old love romances, and
when a happy consummation is not reached we
find the lover remaining true to his lost love, or
the deserted maiden broken-hearted. We are inclined to laugh at all this to-day,—to believe that
because our modern lovers are seldom heroic or
broken-hearted, they were not so in the past;
but we cannot doubt that people once consented

to be burnt at the stake for their faith, because
they would not do this to-day. In the love-story
of Aucassin and Nicolette, of Launcelot and
Guinevere, of Deirdre, and later of Francesca da
Rimini, of Romeo and Juliet, there is little complexity; the love, the passion, was sincere, the
issues plain; the wrong done for the sake of love
had to be expiated, and adultery was not con-
founded with the right of self-expression. Love
was recognised as the most fascinating of themes,
but as in man's interpretation of Nature, only in
modern times has it entered into the depths of
his spirit. The ecstasies of emotion, the

> Infinite passion and the pain
> Of finite hearts that yearn,

the contest between the spirit and the flesh, between the right of fulfilment and expression which
love claims and the recognition of the injury
which that very consummation may inflict on
others,—these things are shown as never before
by our modern writers, and they open gates to
previously unexplored regions of romance.

With gallantry also there has been a passage
from the simple to the complex. In the older
depictions but little was said of its penalties or

cruelties, and the adventures were recorded in the jolliest fashion. Generally they are full of fun as in the story, in *The Golden Ass*, of the cuckold carpenter in the tub, or of May and her lover in the apple tree, or of the Oxford Clerks in *The Canterbury Tales*; and in the *Decameron*, as in the *Contes Drolatiques* the men appeared as good fellows and the ladies merry dames, and no one seemed a bit the worse for the naughtiness. More subtle forms of sexual licence have taken the place of the old ones in our novels and plays, an introduction of a certain spiritual complexity which has made them more alluring and their reactions more disastrous.

One may sometimes wonder whether the world would not have been a pleasanter place if there were no moral restrictions. When we think of the innumerable dreary monogamous lives and the brightness which a change of bed-fellows might have imparted to them; when we think of the lovable women "withering on the virgin thorn" because they cannot marry and dare not have a lover; when we look on the tens of thousands of young men and women longing for love adventure, we may question whether those whose disregard of virtue or whose recklessness allow them to spend week-ends together as lovers are not happier than those whose consciences or fears debar such adventures.

Pleasant and exhilarating in its irresponsibility as the picture may seem of our world without moral restrictions in matters of sex, it would be a retrogression, a step backward towards the conditions of primitive man. It may be seen in force to-day among the people of the South Sea Islands. There, there is no reproach for incontinence, neither is there any professional prostitution. If a girl takes a fancy to a visitor she may become his mistress and return afterwards to her home unashamed, but her favours are not to be bought, except perhaps in some of the islands which have become tainted by commercial civilisation. This is their natural attitude towards sex relations, but where Christianity has been introduced restraints are often recognised. A young man on a ship in which I sailed went ashore on one of the Friendly Islands with the express purpose of amorous adventure. On his return he looked gloomy, and being questioned as to his fortunes replied that he had met a most agreeable young native girl who spoke English excellently and who allowed him to join her in a walk. After a while, as she seemed pleased with his attentions, he made her acquainted with his expectations and received the smiling but firm response, "No, thank you, sir. I am a missionary!" Christianity more than anything else which has uplifted man's moral ideals has made the sex relationship a responsible one; every advance in true civilisation would seem to mark the establishment of a closer bond of union between man and woman, and, with it, graver obligations; and our picture of a world made merrier by sexual irresponsibility must also be one of a civilisation which is unprogressive, or at all events destructive of the ideal of love.

Love has created nobler joys and nobler cares: its ardours are derived from sex, but like a flower whose roots are in the earth it derives its colour from the light of heaven. In a society which has ceased to preserve a standard of sex morality, where the young people indulged in promiscuous unions, no great bonds of love would exist. The sowing of "wild oats" on the part of a man does not promise an ultimate harvest, and in a woman's case any degradation of love is especially harmful. The girls in Europe and America who make week-end excursions with temporary lovers may afterwards marry for love and have children; but has

not the trust which should have been sacred become enfeebled, the passion, which should be
expressed in love, dissipated, the realisation of
their loveliest dreams made impossible? Nevertheless there are cases where the conditions of
modern life justify departure from the accepted
standards of sex morality, and the condemnation
of this departure in the women who are denied
the opportunity of marriage is often cruel and
hypocritical stupidity. A state of protracted vir-
ginity is known to be harmful physically and
mentally to a woman, and her nature is withered
by the denial of motherhood. Every woman who
cannot marry should be allowed to have a lover
and to become a mother without the slightest
shadow falling on her moral character; but in her
choice of a lover moral considerations do arise: she
must love the man and he her, and the relationship must involve no cruelty to others.

The institution of marriage is based on an assumption of fidelity: the religious celebration en-
joins it, the legal conditions make it part of the
contract; but nothing except mutual love can
ensure it. In the Catholic Church marriage is a
sacrament, and this is a magnificent ideal when
it is realised in the union of true lovers; but how

can we so regard it when love is absent, when between the man and woman there is not even comradeship, when he is to her but the provider of a home, she to him but a mistress or house-keeper? The Church makes these unions indissoluble: the law does this also so long as sexual fidelity is maintained, and it seems a preposterous thing that unsympathetic lives should be doomed to enforced alliance. How often have we seen splendid women mated, to quote Stevenson, with "staring burgesses, or white-eyed ferret-faced boys"; or fine men sentenced to life incarceration with "noisy scullions or acidulous vestals", because they chose unwisely in their generous youth? and how often have we wished that there was an escape for them which would neither trouble their own consciences nor awake public censure? How often have we seen the marriage of the ill-mated lead to infidelity? But though the risks of marriage are great and the penalties often severe, on the whole monogamy and the home life accompanying it is the most admirable product of man's social civilisation. For one failure there are a hundred successes. We are inclined to emphasise the exception, and our playwrights and novelists find it so much easier to excite interest in the breach of the Seventh Commandment than in the observance of all the others, that a person who read life from their portrayals of it would conclude that conjugal fidelity was a rare thing. Really it is the solid background of virtue against which these lapses are painted that gives them their significance, just as swearing or obscene language derives its piquancy from the existence of a sense of propriety.

With our love of variety, our response to different expressions of beauty, it is asking a good deal of the wedded that they should remain undisturbed by new sex attractions. Even the austere practitioners of virtuous married life may more often than we think allow their thoughts to be allured by pictures of the forbidden. There is a story of a middle-aged couple, an elder and his wife, returning from the kirk when the minister had been preaching on the wickedness of the sensual life led by Solomon. In the case of the husband the picture given instead of shocking him excited his imagination, and on the walk homeward, after a thoughtful silence, he exclaimed to his wife, "Eh, but it must have been vera plaisant, you know,—Solomon must have had a gra-and time, you know"; to which his wife replied with contempt, "You!" she said, "to be talking about Sōlomon, you wi' your aince a fortnicht!" His wandering fancies naturally irritated her and perhaps she, too, had visions of a merrier wed-bed; but I am sure this couple always remained perfectly faithful to each other. Marriage as a rule is a happy and honest bond, and among the great majority of couples in the races we respect it is a success.

It may seem remarkable that such a large majority of marriages do turn out successfully, when we consider the apparently haphazard fashion in which they are brought about. But perhaps these ways are less haphazard than they look at first sight. When you fall in love Nature is prompting you in your choice, and Nature is a better guide than any selection committee of men and women. In a smile, in a glance, a tone of voice, the lover reads more of the heart than a Coelebs in search of a wife can discover in all his critical tests.

In our endeavour to read and understand the purpose and lessons of life we are not really concerned with man's social laws, except in so far as they embody moral principles and ideals,— indeed the disobedience of legal authority sometimes becomes a duty. In the case of marriage the legal bond is in general accord with the moral ideal and is a working arrangement for which perhaps no substitute could be found; but the bond of true marriage is independent of legal agreements, the legal tie is gradually becoming a weaker one, and as divorce gets easier, the state of legal matrimony may be reduced to the absurdity of the permutations and combinations of bed-fellowship among the cinema actors and actresses of Hollywood. Without a legal bond true marriage would continue and its highest obligations would be fulfilled, but only voluntarily. Love would cease to be protected by the Courts, but would be more securely guarded by honour.

In considering the love between man and woman we may conclude that its best realisation is to be found in a mating which is permanent, not temporary, and that its fullest expression is won not through the stimulus of variety but in the confidence of renewal. But can we ever be sure that we have found our mates,—that after fully believing we had done so, another might not appear who made even a stronger appeal, evoked a deeper devotion? The biographies of some of the most eminent persons, especially of poets and of creative artists, have shown us a succession of loves, each of which in its turn seemed supreme, and even in less imaginative lives the thing occurs. Though the first love may have been genuine, the new love replaces it, and though the temptation to embrace it may be resisted, it remains a reality. And again, a man may marry a second or third time, and be as devoted to and as much enamoured of the young woman he weds in middle age as he was in the case of his first love. It was this complication that led to the question, "In the resurrection whose wife shall she be, for the seven had her?" and was met by a reply hardly satisfactory to those who would believe that the legal or ceremonial bond is eternal.

Love, where sex is not involved, may be constant,—indeed constancy is its truest demonstration,—but sex, which intensifies its expression also threatens its constancy, especially in men. Fidelity in conjugal relations is easier for a woman than for a man. She has less sexual desire and more deterrents; the penalty of unfaithfulness is more severe for her than for him, the loss of a home and of the care of the children a greater deprivation. And also (up to the present time), her virtue stands on a higher level, has more significance than a man's, and in losing it she is (no doubt unjustly) more dishonoured in the eyes of the world. All these things make it easier for her to resist passing temptations. It must also be remembered that a woman loses her sex desires earlier in life than a man; and in the case of married couples the husband may still be virile and susceptible to female magnetism, still capable of attracting women when his wife has lost both her physical charms and her sexual inclinations. Thus we see so many cases of men whose lives had previously been exemplary, "breaking out" when they are over fifty.

The flesh is weak and the spirit seldom unwilling to indulge it. Between man and woman, only when love is based on the firmest foundations can constancy be assured. Happy is he who has found in his mate the object of his desire and the companion of his spirit, and whose love has become a faith.

Sexual desire is often spoken of as an appetite, a hunger that calls for satisfaction; but it differs from the call of the body for food in that it gives while it receives. For our bodily sustenance we consume, we destroy, but in the fulfilment of sex instincts the captive is not a victim, and the possessed becomes also the beneficiary. Though, therefore, we may be depressed or horrified by Nature's scheme for supporting the life of its creatures by its decrees that they shall hunt, slay, and feed upon each other, we may be encouraged by the knowledge that she has improved on this crude procedure in her scheme for the reproduction and continuity of life; at all events in the higher types. If the procreative instinct had inflicted pain and cruelty and destruction on the object of desire instead of promoting its welfare, —if its final expression had been sadism, then, indeed, we might have despaired of the creation of which we are a part; but we may be of good cheer in realising that the final expression of this elemental force is love.

We have been discussing love only in its alliance with and expression through the attraction of sex between man and woman. In all its manifestations,—in the bond between parents and children, between brothers and sisters, or between friends,—love is man's supreme gift and treasure. It has no equivalent, no purchase price:

> What is gold worth, say
> Worth for work or play,
> Worth to keep or pay,

LOVE AND SEX

Hide or throw away,
 Hope about or fear?
What is love worth, pray?
 Worth a tear?

Golden on the mould
Lie the dead leaves rolled
Of the wet woods old,
Yellow leaves and cold,
 Woods without a dove;
Gold is worth but gold;
 Love's worth love.

When love is unrelated to sex it may seem more
unselfish than when the bond is between lovers,
for it is not then dominated by the passion for
exclusive possession. You are not jealous because
your children love or are loved by others. You
welcome, you are not pained by the devotion
another may feel for your friend; but the woman
you love, though she may love another, must not
be *in love* with anyone but yourself, and of course
this applies equally in the case of a woman's
feelings for a man. Sex love demands possession:
the two must belong to each other; and if this is
selfish, it is a state in which self is ennobled and
enlarged, and where the joy of giving is even
greater than that of receiving. Between a man

and woman who are both lovers and friends an intimacy of comradeship is established which cannot be reached in any other relationship. However great the confidence between parent and child, between brothers or sisters, there is always some shyness; and however deep the friendship between one man and another, there is a certain reticence which often forbids them to speak of their inmost thoughts, indeed of their very affection. But in the expression of a passionate love between a man and a woman who are true mates, the barrier between heart and heart is swept away; they *know* each other, and all they know, all that they *like*, all that makes them friends, feeds and renews the flame of their mutual attraction; and, in turn, that physical desire throws a radiance of beauty and gives a thrill of romance to daily life.

In estimating the value of the things that make life happy, we recognise that some of them are transitory and probably depend solely on conditions in our island world, whereas others seem to demand continuity and a faith in their permanence. And chief of all the sources of happiness which seem to have an eternal significance stands love.

Whether or not the spirit of man survive the

body, he has seen in love a vision of the immortal; he feels that love has not expended itself in realisation. It has thrown a light of beauty on the joys and sorrows he has found on Earth, it has awakened aspirations which his years on Earth are inadequate to fulfil, established bonds which they cannot complete; and it has created his nearest approach to a faith that these hopes are not in vain, and these bonds not severed by death.

V

THE INDIVIDUAL

V

THE INDIVIDUAL

FROM the nebulae to the spheres, from the inorganic to the organic, from the lowest plant life to the most complex animal structure, the steps of evolution are marked by ever-increasing individuality in created things; and the latest and greatest of these, of which we have cognisance, the human being, has become conscious of his separate existence and individuality.

Without self-conscious life creation would be meaningless,—without memory to record or reflection to realise, ages might pass, world after world might be created and destroyed, leaving no trace in the universe that they ever existed. The separation of the individual from the rest of life provides the standpoint for observation and contemplation. In the individual, and, as far as we can read, in the individual alone, has life awakened to consciousness of itself.

It is not to be wondered at that the human being is impressed by a sense of his own importance. He finds himself in possession of marvellous powers; he knows no master; he rules the other creatures of the earth, and changes the face of the earth by his labours; and yet a little reflection on the part of the individual will prompt this question,—"How much of this amazing structure which I call myself is *I*, I who have awakened into life but had no part in my own creation? Is not everything that expresses me in body and mind an inheritance from my ancestors?"

Though he may not belong to the class of persons whose family tree is preserved, he has as many ancestors as if he knew his pedigree, and may well feel bewildered by the thought of their number. If every marriage of two people produced four children (and though this may be above the present average it is below the historic records), a man of to-day would have about a million ancestors living in the tenth century if there had been no inter-family marriages. It would be difficult to make even an approximate estimate of the true numbers, but probably a hundred thousand would be near the mark. The individual is a resultant, but not necessarily a compound of all his ancestors. He does not inherit their qualities in equal measure. There is what is called "the impressive sire", a procreator who stamps his individuality on a family; and also, though perhaps not so often, there are impressive mothers. Constantly in a family generations are skipped, and records of character, or portraits, show a recurrence of likeness, a greater similarity between grandparents and grandchildren than between parents and child; and sometimes a marked revival of the traits of a more distant ancestor.

The individual may be proud of his forefathers and inclined to talk about them if they were distinguished people; or if he does not know who his great-grandfather was, or does know that he was an insignificant member of society, he may regard references to pedigrees as snobbish; but in any case when he is inclined to be vainglorious about himself and his own performances, he should be brought back to the question,—"How much of this personality of mine is ME? Am I anything but the resultant of those lives which preceded mine,—lives which I had no part myself in shaping? Is this ego something independent of the mental and bodily characteristics inherited from my ancestors, or is it also a transmission? Can I not even call my soul my own?"

If this consciousness that I am I is inherited

from our ancestors, then we *are* our ancestors: we have lived before and forgotten our former lives. If "the inevitable me" was as much derived from a forefather as the colour of our eyes, then I am that forefather re-embodied. If, on the other hand, though our characteristics be inherited, the ego, the selfhood of each of us, was not inherited, then a separate creature, something new in life, has awakened with each individual birth.

Let us examine both these possibilities. Throughout his life a man's body and mind undergo modifications; his opinions, his tastes, his very principles change; but from childhood to old age he is conscious of being the same person. There would be nothing unreasonable, therefore, in imagining that what happens from decade to decade might be extended from life to life, and that though he had forgotten his pre-existence as completely as he has forgotten his infancy, he might be an ancestor re-embodied, with tastes and characteristics perhaps quite different, but with the same ego. If this reading of the design of life be true, it would remove the injustice of the hereditary transmission of defects, and it would also relieve the individual from the humiliation of feeling that he is no more than the obedient product of his forefathers' activities. "He visits the sins of the fathers upon the children!" We have seen that this is so, and have felt its injustice. A man is a drunkard or contracts venereal disease, and his descendants suffer for it in mental and bodily defects; but suppose the descendant *is* the forefather who sinned, then he has been the author of his punishment as much as he would be by delinquencies in his present life.

The idea is rather cynically expressed in these verses:

Blame not your ancestors that you inherit
From them the sins and pains you do not merit.
Ye are your own forefathers and begetters
Of all the ills that hold your souls in fetters.
To love thy neighbour as thyself were wise,
Because he is thyself but in disguise.
If thou and he could but exchange your skins,
Ye might dislike each other's loves and sins,
And see no more the world ye look on now,
But he would still be he, and thou be thou.
Each is the keeper of the other's life,
Or else the robber of the other's store;
And when thou liest with thy neighbour's wife
Thou art the cuckold and thy wife the whore.[1]

In the happier aspect of the picture, the healthy

[1] *The Immortal Jew.*
115

and upright would become their own bene-
factors.

If we have lived before in our ancestors, we
have no memory of it; but it is possible to imagine in the course of further evolution, a superman of the future whose memory would be
pre-natal, and who would be able to recall his
ancestral embodiments.

The alternative theory involves the belief that
though physical and mental characteristics are
inherited from an ancestor, each individual is a
separate and new creation; that however like an
ancestor you may be, you are not *he*; that an ego
which was not contained in any forefather, and
will not survive in any descendant, has appeared
in the universe. Something has *begun*. Hydrogen
and oxygen combine and form water; blue and
yellow are fused and produce green; independent
personalities may unite and bring forth another
which has its own individuality,—an ego which
has had no pre-existence.

Now whether we accept either of these views
or reject them both, we are brought back to our
first question,—how much of a man's personality
can he claim to be *himself*? Has he any self apart
from that which has been transmitted from his

ancestors? The determinist will say, "None"; he will maintain that every activity, every taste on which a man prides himself, is inherited; that he acts wisely or foolishly, nobly or basely, in obedience to qualities which have been bequeathed to him; and if we ask,—Has he not the will to choose between two courses, perceiving that one is good and the other bad? the determinist will reply that this very exercise of will is inherited and inevitable. If this be true, it relieves the individual of all responsibility, and it is not the murderer, not even his basest forefather, who should be hanged, for he, poor devil, would be able to throw the blame on a remoter ancestor, and we should then be lost in the intricacies of an eternal pedigree.

The contention of the determinist may nevertheless be true: it is difficult to disprove it, and yet there is a persistent conviction in the human mind that man *has* the power of choice and *is* responsible for his actions. The holder of this conviction may admit that his artistic tastes, his preferences in literature or music or wine, his skill in physical accomplishments, his mental abilities, are mainly inherited from his forbears; he may even admit that his views as to what is right and wrong may be largely inherited, but when it comes to a decision between *doing* right or wrong he feels that it is he himself who makes that decision, that the choice, which may be either an acceptance of the easier course or one requiring effort or sacrifice, is his own.

He may know that he has inherited a certain weakness of character, and yet determine that he will not be the servant of that weakness but will conquer it, and he will maintain that in the exercise of that choice he finds and proves *himself*.

Himself! but whence and what this freedom? We must always look for origins; we cannot conceive of anything self-created,—springing into existence from nothing. If our reflections have brought us to the belief that we have no power of choice, we must look for the origin of the self-conscious individual and that individual's conduct in a Creator of automata, or in the elemental chemical laboratories: if we believe that we have the freedom and power of choice, we must seek its source in the entrance into our spirits of the creative power itself.

The individual whose qualities of mind and body are admittedly derived from his ancestors,

118

but who nevertheless feels that his soul is his own, is like the inheritor of an entailed property, of lands and house and furniture. He lives in these surroundings and his life is influenced by them; they are passed on to his heir; but before he dies he sets his mark on them. He may alter the furniture, restore the buildings, improve the cultivation of the land,—or, he may cut down the woods and allow the place to fall into ruin. Whether it be his home and lands or his own body and spirit that a man takes care of or neglects, his heir will feel the consequences as well as himself. The third and fourth generation of those who follow will feel the benefit of his wisdom and truth of choice or the penalty of his follies and selfishness. So may a man be said to hold his life in trust for the future generations: if it be not his own soul that he bequeaths it is the structure through which the future souls will be expressed, the house that may be a pleasant home or a prison; and, as I have suggested, he may be his own forefather, his own heir.

The individual soul, limited as it is by its immediate surroundings, would seem to have illimitable capacities for enlargement. The self, which is self-absorbed, occupied only with its pleasures or interests, is fulfilled in self, like seed unsown. In sympathy with others, in work, in admiration and love, it sows its life beyond itself, and becomes part of a larger life. Even in connection with places, the affection for the homeland, the appreciation of beautiful scenes, almost incorporates us into those scenes, and a man is ennobled by every lovely thing that touches his heart. And this is still more so in his human fellowship: he finds *himself* in friendship and love: in giving he receives. The measure of the soul is its capacity for sympathy, and the wider its horizons extend beyond the gates of self, the greater his inheritance.

The human being is indeed an amazing composition:—his body a part of the Earth's substance, akin to plant and animal (indeed containing most of the elements known to chemical science), his senses and intelligence a gradual evolution through which an incomprehensible creative force is expressing itself in temporal manifestations, and his self-conscious spirit something added to or emergent from these,—a new appearance in creation, a person who controls the structure in which he is incarnated, who in separation from other life becomes able to realise life, and by sympathy, effort, and the exercise of choice can enlarge his whole being. This is the individual soul, the most enduring, and as far as we know the ultimate expression of life.

Each of us is conscious of his individual life and cannot explain it; he asks himself why he is *he* and not another; each of us feels that he is "the inevitable ME", and I have sometimes thought that this ego of which each of us is aware is the same in all of us. If, for instance, you and another man are together in a room, it is generally accepted as obvious that you are two different people in the same room; but I think it is probable that if you could change places you would find that you were each the same conscious person, but in a different room,—that you would be a person with other tastes and opinions, in a room where everything looked strange, but you, the beholder, the you who was conscious of yourself, would not be essentially changed, or, if changed, that it would be no more so than the modification which takes place in the conscious ego at different periods of life. The conception that every individual ego is the same,—here moving towards a higher phase of life, there lapsing towards extinction,—may throw a light on the mystery of individuality, and on the reality of human brotherhood.

In speaking of the conscious ego I have assumed that this remains constant in the individual, that though he changes from year to year, from youth to age in a hundred ways, he, the conscious self, always remains one, that it is the same I who felt pleasure or pain as a child who suffers or rejoices as a man, the same I who knew he had done something naughty as a boy who is pricked by conscience in maturity. But are we sure that this is so? While sure that I am *one* with my past self, may I not be conscious of growth, of expansion or deterioration not only in my physical and mental qualities but in the very ego that is conscious of them? In one direction at least I believe that this is so. Whenever the power of choice is exercised morally, whenever we must decide between what we feel to be right and wrong, whenever our courage is put to proof or an achievement calls for effort, something is changed, added to, or taken from the soul by our decision, and we know this. Our realisation not only of the world around us but of our inmost self is changed,—is ennobled or degraded.

Let us, however, be thankful if we have made

the finer choice that our victory does not promote
in us vainglory or intolerance which would again
shut the gates of self upon our humanity; and let
us hope, when we fail and have to bear the
penalties of failure, that this may not harden our
hearts, but give us sympathy for others who have
also been defeated.

It was the conviction that the individual is
something more than the obedient resultant of
ancestral lives, and has freedom of choice that
inspired Henley to write the lines,

> I am the master of my fate;
> I am the captain of my soul.

The assertion in the first line is not true. No
man is master of his fate, though he may help to
decide it. Henley was fated by his pedigree to
endure the miseries of illness over which he had
no control; but of the soul that bore those suffer-
ings heroically he was the captain. The ship was
leaking, and storm-battered, but there was a
seaman steering her until she either foundered or
reached haven.

The power of choice is, as I said, the only part
of our personality that we can really call "our-
self". If we did not possess it we should be

machines, automata obedient to the elemental forces, creatures in bondage to irresponsible passions and appetites. The consciousness of responsibility, of choice between good and evil, the faith that life itself is in our care, brings the human soul into comradeship with a Divine Presence, into co-operation with an immortal purpose.

In this power of choice man becomes a living Soul, launched on the great adventure of life with limitless scope for achievement on the one hand, and on the other a penalty,—the penalty of death.

The self-conscious individual is the highest and most comprehensive manifestation of life we know of. The conception of certain religions that after death the individual life is absorbed into the life-spirit from which it emerged, the belief in Nirvana, is a belief in retrogression, a process comparable to that of the dissipation of worlds and systems into the nebulous gases from which they were evolved. If we are to imagine a continued evolution of life, it must be in the enlargement of the individual, through finer sympathies and greater self-control, to a truer self-realisation, a wider freedom. Not in the absorption of the

124

individual into the Spiritual Whole, not in dissolution of the house of Life, but in its strengthening and beautifying, does the Divine Soul enter into the human.

A world, a universe of life without self-conscious independent individuals, would be like a stage of shifting scenes without actors, or with actors who were puppets. The only life which has reality is manifested through the individual. All meaning is held in personality. From the relationship to each other of our separate lives spring all life's interests, its tragedies, its comedies, its loves and hatreds. The individual possesses the glorious power of giving, and of forgiving; he may even sacrifice himself, or herself (perhaps more often), for the good of another. Through the separateness of independent personalities comes the bond of comradeship, and the most beautiful of all life's manifestations, love.

It is almost impossible for our minds to reconcile the phenomena of time and space with any conception we may attempt of the timeless and unbounded. Our bodies, our senses, our minds are creations of time, and we can to some extent understand and think about them; but the self-conscious soul seems to have conceptions and aspirations beyond the scope of the structure it inhabits, to realise an independence of that structure, and a connection with the permanent. No flight of the imagination can lead us to a solution of the mystery of our being. We must be content to learn what we can of its purpose and responsibilities within our temporary boundaries, and endeavour to enlarge those boundaries beyond the gates of self.

VI

GOOD AND EVIL

VI

GOOD AND EVIL

As a general definition of good and evil we may say that the good is that which is productive and evil that which is destructive of life; and, as a corollary, that the good is measurable by its power to lift life from lower to higher levels, and evil by its power to degrade it. These oppositions indicate in one direction continued progress, in the other final conclusions; for the good is creative and we can imagine no bounds to the possibilities of life, but evil is destructive and its goal is death.

In our reading of Nature we have seen only one thing which suggests that evil may be a positive force, inherent in life, and that is the predatory instinct, the destruction of one life by another in its own interest. In unself-conscious life, where there can be no moral responsibility, we see forces which are helpful or hostile to evolutionary progress, and we may regard them thus as good or evil, but it is only in the self-conscious life in man that these become transmuted into right and wrong. To consider unself-conscious life first: accompanying its magnificent and beautiful embodiments, we see a condition which makes one creature actually dependent for its existence on the destruction of another. This decree of being, and the pain it involves, is to man's moral sense unjust and cruel. But can it be called evil? According to our definition it would only be so when it threatened the evolutionary progress of life; and as no moral precept can apply to the unself-conscious, its character can only be estimated by its results. If we can discover anywhere in Nature processes which have in them the seeds of degradation;—if disease, for instance, is essential and inevitable, and not accidental and preventible, we may call that evil; but I do not think there is evidence of any such malign constituent in life; and if the harsh methods of Nature lead to the development of higher forms of life, though our moral sense may consider them inhumane, we cannot describe them as evil.

We see that there are elemental forces operating irresponsibly,—a life force striving for expression and self-assertion, and emergent from, or above and beyond these, a conscious will and effort revealed through the spirit of man. These elemental natural forces, these blind self-assertive life movements are to the creative spirit what the sea waves are to the swimmer, what the wind is to the bird that develops wings to rise against it, what an untamed horse is to the rider. Unguided, misguided, these forces take the line of least resistance and may become destructive; but allied with and inspired by the spirit their impetus and potentialities win the great victories of creation.

The introduction of a creative purpose and will may seem to some thinkers a pure assumption. It exists without doubt in man's ideals and actions, but at what stage of his evolution from the lower animal this spiritual force became part of him we are ignorant. We may believe that its appearance is a tragical, or even humorous, accident of innumerable permutations and combinations of atomic gambols, or,—that "God breathed into his nostrils the breath of life and man became a living soul". The former belief would leave the question of good and evil, right and wrong, one for the laboratory, the latter would bring it into the court of eternal justice. Whatever its parentage, the human spirit with its perception of right and wrong is a reality, and its power of choice between good and evil seems to be an endowment which was not derived from chemical affinities.

Though, then, we may hold different views as to the sources of good and evil, these views or beliefs cannot but influence our conduct. The same actions have different meanings according to the motives which direct them: a gift may be made in pure love or in self-interest; and in going into battle, though a soldier may fight as bravely in a bad cause as a good one, the spirit in which he looks for victory or faces death is very different when he is fighting for the honour or in defence of his country, from that which is felt by a mercenary.

And so in facing the practical problems of life, our confidence, our exhilaration, our fighting power, will be stimulated by a faith that there is a purpose in our efforts and that they are inspired by and in co-operation with a divine purpose, as they could not be if we believed that the performances of duties were but the outcome of our recognition of the ascertained effects of certain lines of conduct.

Self, or "selfhood" as Robert Bridges enlarges the meaning of the word, is a realisation of life and is a necessity for its operation. Let us try to picture a world of conscious beings in which the self was suppressed,—a state of altruism carried to extremes. It would be like a cricket match, in which the bowler instead of trying to take the batsman's wicket, sent him an easy half-volley, and the batsman instead of hitting it to the boundary, spooned it into the hands of a fielder, who in turn out of consideration for the feelings of the batsman, dropped the catch. The game of life played in this way would be equally foolish. In both games the keener the opposition the better, and the antagonism need never be coupled with ill-will. Self is essential in life and may be allied with good or evil: it is then expressed as right or wrong, sin or virtue.

Accepting the definition that the good is that which preserves and uplifts life and the evil that which degrades and destroys it, man, who finds himself influenced by and often definitely in control of this force, thus becomes the caretaker or enemy of life itself.

This magnificent privilege and responsibility of man brings with it burdens and penalties, but it does not forbid, indeed it commands as a duty, his enjoyment of life. He must love the life he would guard and uplift. He must "cherish it in every fibre" of his being; its warm passions must not be distrusted. The more ardently he can feel, and guide, and express through his conscious self the vitality of the unconscious forces, the greater will be the advance of the powers of life over death.

To find happiness is the first function of man: to find happiness for himself without injuring the happiness of any other is his first duty: to create happiness for others is his highest duty.

The perception of good and evil (in other words of that which is beneficial or harmful to life) is no doubt a faculty of the intelligence which has been gradually evolved. But man possesses a moral faculty beyond this *recognition* of good and evil, namely, the consciousness of his power to choose between them. This freedom is probably his highest endowment: it lifts him to a plane of life beyond that of the automata; it is the only part of him which is not determined by inheritance. The exercise of moral choice does not seem to be the outcome of experience or calculation but to be influenced by faith in an absolute principle,—it may indeed demand conduct which may be contrary to the teaching of experience, and adverse to his own interests. Man's noblest and kindest qualities seem to have been inspired by this faith in the right rather than by his calculation of consequences. They are not intellectual products. Every virtue,—honour, courage, kindness, self-sacrifice,—is as evident among simple and un-intellectual people as in those of the highest mental capacity. If the moral nature were an intellectual evolution the qualities we should most highly esteem would be utilitarian: caution would be more approved than heroism; self-interest would seem a finer thing than self-sacrifice; love would be distrusted as an obscurer of clear vision and rational conduct, and expediency would be the measure of virtue. We should also expect to find that the men of greatest intellect were those of greatest rectitude, but they are no nobler than others, and we have men of Bacon's capacity who can be described as the wisest and yet the meanest of mankind.

A community evolved through purely intellectual processes would probably be like one of those grotesque scientific Utopias imagined by Mr. Wells or Mr. Bernard Shaw, or the uglier new world of Mr. Aldous Huxley's forecast where love is superseded by lust and human life propagated in a laboratory.

No intellectual theory which is opposed to the kind instincts of the human heart can endure;

but the most virtuous intentions may often do harm when they are pursued in opposition to the reason. The essential good—kindness—stands every test; and it will be clear that though the intention may be conscientious, as at times in religious persecution, the act is bad because it is not based upon the instinct of kindness, but misdirected by mental confusion.

Though the intellect may not be the source of the moral sense, these two are allies not opponents, and it is only when they are working together that the great movements of human progress are achieved.

The suggested definition of evil as that which degrades or is destructive of life may help us in the examination of a question which we cannot help asking, namely, whether a certain amount of what has generally been classed as evil is not a desirable thing,—whether without it life would not be a very tame affair. Evil is always loathsome or cruel or mean. The rebellious Satan of tradition is no embodiment of evil; the cunning and cynical Mephistopheles, though coming nearer to its representation than the fallen angel of Milton, is not wholly despicable. Creative imagination has not yet given us a personification of the greedy, cruel, and obscene monster which would embody what we know as really evil.

Evil is the enemy not only of life but of everything that makes life worth having. The evil which we speak of as adding a flavour to life is never loathsome or mean or cruel,—indeed it will be found on examination to have qualities to which the term evil is inapplicable, qualities which are often heroic, and which, though they may be defiant of accepted standards of morality, involve in their exercise both courage and sacrifice. The wickedness, the "spice of the devil", the qualities we welcome or condone as adding to the interest of life, are generally an expression of exuberant vitality, an exhibition of energies good in themselves, but perhaps thoughtlessly displayed or allowed to get out of hand, and these are generally associated with the young. In a man they show themselves in a disregard for authority, in a recklessness of consequences in pursuit of his passionate impulses; in a woman the condonable wickedness is to be found in her possession of an extra endowment of sex attractiveness which she exercises imprudently or disastrously. But in neither case, unless these qualities are coupled with meanness, vanity, or disloyalty, can they be damned as evil. They are good qualities lacking discipline; and when we say that an admixture of evil adds to the interest and gaiety of life, let us remember our definition of evil.

As far as it is possible for man to read the mystery of life and discover its meaning and intent, the clearest light he has found comes through the medium of his moral nature. Mental capacity is a matter of degree, intellectual achievements but steps on the way towards enlightenment; but in the moral law we find truth itself. Among human beings we see ranges of mental power in which one individual is almost as far removed from another as the savage from the ape. We can picture inhabitants of a greater sphere than the earth whose intellectual equipment might be to man's what man's is to an insect's. To them the most complex mathematical problem would be as self-evident as we find a sum in simple arithmetic, and the enigmas of time and space that "tease us out of thought" would present no difficulties. But in such a sphere we cannot imagine its superman capable of any deed nobler than one which may be done by a human being. A life of devotion to a great ideal, a simple deed of kindness, an act of heroic self-sacrifice, are

138

as great and complete as anything we can conceive: they are not measurable or relative; they are absolute and conclusive. We have been shown in the moral law a truth which seems applicable to universal life, and may be accepted as the surest guide to its interpretation.

The natural capacity of man for the performance of good or bad actions, equally with his intellectual endowments, is inherited: the use of these qualities, their cultivation or neglect, the *choice*, is the individual's contribution to life.

Truth is an eternal reality: untruth has no reality. Beauty is a manifestation of harmony in life, ugliness of discord. Love is the creator of bonds that strengthen, hatred of severances that enfeeble. Light and air have reality, darkness and vacuums have none. In relation to life all these negatives are hostile. Though there is no such reality as untruth, falsehood is the most insidious enemy of human happiness and progress; and, though hatred and cruelty and uncleanness are not independent forces but deficiencies, so horrible, so tyrannous are their effects that it is not to be wondered at that man has conceived of evil as well as good as a positive power, and has seen visions not only of God and Heaven but of Satan and Hell. But though we may be unable now to believe in Apollyon or the Father of Lies, or hold that evil as well as good has an eternal source;— though we see the goal of evil not in the punishment of Hell but in the dissolution of death, it is none the less the perennial enemy. The conflict of the drift, the falsehood, the indifference, the self-aggrandisement, the cruelty, against the purpose, the effort, the courage, the sacrifice,—between all that mars the beauty of life and all that promotes it, is one in which we are forever engaged. Every deed and choice of man is either helping to preserve life and carry it onward to happy issues or is hindering its labours and obscuring its light. Death, not Hell, is the doom of defeat; but what greater cause could man have to fight for than the vindication of life itself,— what more awful enemy than annihilation?

If we are indeed such stuff as dreams are made of,—if our selfhoods are not to be annihilated, if we are sharers in a purpose extending beyond our years on earth, then our reading of life points to a gradual extension of our mental capacity, to expanding horizons of intellectual adventure, to greater mastery over the material elements of the universe, to the quest of knowledge over the uncharted seas that lie beyond our island shores; but transcending this knowledge which we seek, is a truth which we carry with us, the compass of moral truth, which knows no deflection, and whose polarity is the love we have found on earth and may believe to be eternal and divine.

✻　　✻　　✻

Inherited from the remotest past, mingled with and again freeing itself from a thousand grotesque superstitions, filtered through the ages, man's belief in God has persisted. The more primitive his conception of God the more material has been its expression. At first it was embodied in the graven image, the idols which in themselves became objects of worship: in later presentations the idea of God appears through incarnations in human form. In the modern world where reason has been used in the light of scientific knowledge and the miraculous set aside, the conception of God has been a presence that we know through his attributes, whose purpose we can share through our labours, whose happiness we can enter into in our appreciation of the earth's beauty, and whose love we can realise in the love of our fellow creatures.

If those activities of the elemental forces of Nature which primitive man, unable to understand, regarded as direct manifestations of deity, have been explained by modern science, the mystery of life itself is as far away as ever from his comprehension: if the evolution of man's moral faculties has been traced by physiology and psychology, the inspiration which directs all moral effort still asks for his faith in a supernatural source.

All man's intellectual standards are relative: in his moral conceptions, in his idea of God, he recognises the absolute. The super-beings of another sphere might have mental capacities immeasurably greater than man's, but they would not be to man as gods. The very greatness of such beings would separate them from man: they and man could understand each other no better than men and ants; but man's conception of God is of an infinite sympathy and understanding in which the humblest effort finds itself recognised.

We do not deride scientific methods because there were absurdities in the scientific conclusions of past ages, or condemn modern medical treatment because of the grotesque remedies of previous generations; nor should we distrust the

142

conception of Deity, which has emerged from crude primitive gropings in search of truth, because of the delusions which preceded it. The origin and growth of the religions of mankind is too vast a subject to be entered into here, and indeed it is not essential in the reading of life I am attempting. The idea of God which I am considering is that which has survived all superstitious or dogmatic creeds, and can not only satisfy man's noblest imaginings, but also be acceptable to his reason.

A persistent conception of God is that of the omnipotent creator,—the creator not only of the earth and man, but of the whole universe,—of a creator who is not only all-powerful, but the source of all goodness. Here reason is faced with a difficulty. If God created everything He created what we call evil. To say that He did not create evil but allowed it, is a definite evasion. Even if it were maintained that evil was a necessity for the creation and trial of a human soul, it would have to be admitted that the evil was part of God's creation. How can we accept such a conclusion? Look for a moment at a few of the manifestations of evil,—the cruelty in Nature, the destruction of the weaker creature by the stronger for sustenance and the tortures involved in that process, the inhumanity of man, the frightful accompaniments of war, the horror of epidemics, the injustice of the transmission of disease from parents to offspring! Who can believe that all this is part of a beneficent Creator's design of life? but if we refuse to believe it we must also refuse to believe that He is the omnipotent Creator.

The alternative is to believe that God is not the inventor of evil but the protest against it: that He is not the Creator of life but its *Re-creator*: that not only is the individual soul, as taught by Christ, born again, but life itself is regenerated through God.

The universe of an omnipotent creator would be automatic in obedience to his will, the last action of any living creature determined by the first cause; and the existence of individual souls with freedom of choice would be impossible.

The idea of an all-powerful creator who is not all-beneficent, or of what Carlyle called "a cold absentee God", or of Sir J. Jeans's Divine Mathematician, of any God who is not a sympathetic living presence, cannot be accepted by the human spirit. To no such Deity could man give devotion.

But in a, to man, incomprehensible universe, he can accept the idea of a spirit which does comprehend it; amid chaotic elemental forces he can imagine the inspiration of a transcendent purpose; he could give devotion to a God who is the fountain source of all effort, of all goodness and beauty, the uplifter of life, the protest against wrong. In him man would see, not an omnipotent creator whose work was completed, but one whose labours are continuous, whose harvest fields are unbounded.

There has been no greater conception by the human mind than that of justice. Man has not learned it from Nature, where he sees, almost everywhere, conflictions with his sense of justice. He can believe that his own sense of it may be faulty, that in his temporal life it is unattainable, but, nevertheless, his ideal of absolute justice remains unshaken.

In his recognition of justice man's reason tells him that when he does wrong and is punished for the wrong, this is just; that if he deliberately injures another for what appears to be his own advantage, and suffers in spiritual degradation as a consequence, this is just; and when a wrong is done to himself, the feeling is intensified and he is eager to be the instrument of inflicting the punishment. This would be justice. But here another quality is revealed to his spirit, namely, forgiveness. This is irrational, but above reason: Sir J. Jeans's Divine Mathematician could not consider it. Man realises also that when personal punishment follows sin the burden has been laid on the right shoulders; but here again comes an appeal to a higher court. The burden has been laid on the right shoulders, but the lifting of that burden by another on to his own shoulders is an event which transcends justice.

In the reconciliation of perfect justice with forgiveness, of power with self-sacrifice, the Christian religion has given to man his noblest conception of God.

To feel that the universe of life is not a mechanism, shaped or shattered by purposeless forces, or manufactured by omnipotence, but a scene of infinite adventure in which there is a leader, a battlefield of effort against drift in which there is a protagonist, is to realise the presence of a living God. In a universe where everything was preordained by omnipotence, man's efforts would have no ultimate effect; in a universe which God lives to inspire and uplift, every action is of

moment, every triumph or defeat has a consequence, every thought an eternal significance.
Man, no longer an automaton but a sharer in
the divine labours, becomes a contributor or a
hindrance to the great commonwealth of life,
not a mere recipient of its doles; and everything
in creation that would be otherwise ephemeral
acquires a permanent value. And man would
recognise God, not in his isolated omnipotence
but in his vast humanity.

Conscious human personality is the highest
manifestation of life we know of. This is to the
unconscious life as the sphered worlds are to the
gaseous nebulae; and the Oriental conception of
God as an all-pervading spirit into which the
individual life is absorbed after death is an imaginative retrogression, not an advance, and is
comparable to a dissolution of created worlds into
their constituent atoms. Rather should we conceive of God as the supreme Personality which
realises itself in universal sympathy and from
which all individual selfs derive their light.

Men cannot visualise God as a person, and yet
he can only feel His reality in a consciousness of
His personal presence. Man cannot give loyalty
to an abstraction; he can feel no more love for

the idea of omnipotence than for the second law of thermodynamics. If God exists He is revealed to man in the human spirit, in the reading of his own heart and those of his fellow creatures. "There is", said Sir Thomas Browne, "a piece of divinity in us, something that was before the elements, and owes no homage to the sun."

While recognising all its own shortcomings and compromises, the spirit of man has felt that truth and justice *are* realities, and has conceived God as their ultimate foundation. To quote from an article by Miss Cicely Hamilton which expresses this belief in better words than I can find, "Whatever else the acceptance of God may mean in our lives, this it does mean: that there is a Being,— call it what you will,—to whom it is impossible to lie. Of none among men can that 'impossible' be said . . . to lift up your heart to God, even for a moment, is to place yourself for that moment in a presence that annihilates deceit."

The conviction of a divine presence which men have found in prayer, in the fulfilment of duty, in the love of others, cannot be ignored by those who have not had this experience. There is, indeed, no other evidence so strong in support of the existence of God as the benediction this faith brings, and its influence on human conduct. Scientific knowledge shows no egress for the human spirit from the body, no eternal treasury in which the beauty of the earth and the achievements of man may be preserved when the fabric of the earth itself is destroyed. The existence of God, the bond between His spirit and man's, is the only link between the temporary and the abiding, between mortality and permanence.

We are travellers on an unknown way, fascinated by the mystery and wonder of the life around us, happy in sharing its activities; and we are seekers after truth, gathering fragments of knowledge as we go; but if we are to believe that all that we find worth living for is not a delusion, we must look beyond our knowledge and trust to the larger vision of our inspired moments, as foresights of imperishable realities.

The refusal to allow the limitations of our knowledge to belittle our noblest conception of life's meaning is faith. Separated from reason faith becomes credulity. Reason is not opposed to faith. Faith is reason on the wings of hope. Faith is not an endowment, it is a discovery: it is not a virtue, though the conduct which leads to it may be a virtue,—it is a reward.

The spirit may be willing but the flesh is weak, and few of us can hold a faith which is securely anchored. I believe, however, that it is a common human experience that every effort a man makes in a direction he feels to be right, every act of courage, every attempt to set the crooked straight, or to save others, brings him to a firmer faith in life and in a great purpose inspiring it.

We are travellers on an unknown way, every step beyond us unexplored, every vista new. At times the incomprehensible mystery of it all overwhelms us. We look up into the vast depths of the heavens and read no sign: we explore the microcosms on the earth, the alien communities of the insect world, and we find no help to a solution; and yet, in the beauty of a flower, in the love of a fellow creature, we seem to be near a clue to the secret.

Among the imaginings of man there is none more full of despair than that which Maeterlinck suggests as a possibility,—namely, that there *is* no solution. But though no knowledge attainable by man can ever discover the mystery and meaning of existence, his reason tells him that there must be a solution; and in the illumination of his spirit he has felt that the solution is God.

VII

OLD AGE AND DEATH

VII

OLD AGE AND DEATH

THE duration of human lives on Earth seems to have been adjusted to the Earth's dimensions. A prolongation of the term of individual life would mean a restriction in succession. Whatever our views may be as to our fitness to inhabit a larger sphere of life, and enter into greater experiences than this world allows us, we have to recognise that as dwellers here our three score and ten, or four score years is as long a time as the conditions make practicable. All the Utopias assume unlimited room. I suppose Mr. Bernard Shaw's Methuselahs would go on procreating, but if such prolonged activities took place on Earth, congestion would before long make it uninhabitable.

It is hardly worth while to allow our imaginations to play with the picture of life on Earth under different natural conditions than those which we have to obey. If we may amuse ourselves by doing this the ideal would seem to be found in the curtailment rather than the extension of the term of human life. There would be no old age. Men, instead of declining gradually from the maturity of their powers to enfeeblement, and dying when they had reached their lowest level, would die at the zenith of their capacities, women when they had arrived at the fullest expression of their beauty. Such a picture is pleasanter than that of a community chiefly composed of wise patriarchs who had "outgrown their troublesome desires", and virile elders who still had an eye on the Susannahs.

Though we may resent the disabilities of old age, we can see its uses. If we had to leave the earth just when everything was at its best with us instead of at its worst we should find the dismissal much harder to bear, and death would become a more imminent fear. Whatever may be possible in other parts of the universe, old age and death are necessary accompaniments of human life on Earth and we must accommodate ourselves to them as best we can.

In reading the lessons of childhood we have been impressed by the felicity of the gradations through which we become acquainted with the tremendous spectacle of life,—a wonder which if presented to us suddenly when our powers were mature would probably prove an unbearable shock; and so, by a similar gradation from maturity to old age, in the loss of energy, the desire for rest, we are brought to our realisation of death.

Old age has the special advantage of the lessons of experience. Reason and calm judgment should have fuller scope when the warm passions and violent prejudices of youth are left behind. Serene contemplation of life as a whole should replace its anxieties and ambitions. This is the view which Cicero expresses in *De Senectute*, where he maintains that the rational and contemplative satisfactions of age contribute more to a state of true happiness than the excitements and pleasures of youth. He says:

They advance no argument of any weight who say that old age is not actively employed, and resemble those who would assert that the pilot is not employed in navigation when some are climbing the masts, others running up and down the decks, others pumping out the bilge water, while the mariner sits at his ease at the stern holding the rudder. He may not be doing what the young men do, but in truth he is much more arduously and much more profitably engaged.

And he proceeds to describe the pleasures of contemplation and observation, the satisfaction which comes of aims fulfilled and the honour earned by achievement, and the special opportunities for enjoying the study of nature and country pursuits; all of which, he claims, are the special heritage of the old. He makes, however, the provision in his praise of old age, that it must be founded on a well-conducted youth, and that only honourable deportment in the earlier part of life can reap a harvest of reverence at its close.

Montaigne's view is very different. He goes to the other extreme in his estimate of the capacities of youth and age. He says:

I believe our souls are adult at twenty as much as they are ever likely to be and as capable then as ever;

and again:

Of all the great human actions I ever heard or read of, of what sort soever, more were performed before the age of thirty than after;

and he adds of his own personal experience:

I do believe that since that age both my understanding and my constitution have rather decayed than improved. 'Tis possible that with those who make the best use of their time, knowledge and experience may increase with their years; but vivacity, promptitude, steadiness and other pieces of us, of much greater importance, and much more essentially our own, languish and decay.

This is a strange commentary from the profound scholar whose best work was done in middle age.

Goldsmith in the *Citizen of the World* says that age lessens our enjoyment of life but increases our desire of living,—that when we are old life has nothing to recommend it but becomes endeared to us by familiarity and the mere habit of living. Stevenson in his delightful essay, *Crabbed Age and Youth*, gives youth the credit for a finer and even wiser outlook on life than age. With age he associates the cowardly and prudential maxims.

The opinions of old men about life [he says] have been accepted as final. All sorts of allowances are made for the illusions of youth, and none, or almost none for the disenchantments of age. It is held to be a good taunt and somehow or other to clinch the question when an old gentleman waggles his head and says, "Ah! so I thought when I was your age". It is not thought an answer at all if the young man retorts, "My venerable Sir, so I shall probably think when I am yours".

As to the superior discretion of age he says:

Perhaps the want of power has more to do with the wise resolutions of age than we are always inclined to

admit. It would be an instructive experiment to make
an old man young again and leave him all his *savoir*. I
scarcely think he would put his money in the Savings
Bank after all; I doubt if he would be such an admirable son as we are led to expect; and as to his conduct
in love, I believe firmly he would out-Herod Herod,
and put the whole of his new compeers to the blush.

And now hear Browning:

Grow old along with me!
The best is yet to be,
The last of life, for which the first was made:
Our times are in His hand
Who saith, "A whole I planned",
Youth shows but half: trust God: see all, nor be afraid.

He here claims a *magnitude* for old age which is
denied to youth, a wisdom won from the vision
of life as a whole rather than in its sections; but
he also assumes that the vision is received with
a faith in the value of the whole.

Faith in God is undoubtedly the greatest help
old age can have, but it is this faith, won in the
battle of life, not the old age, that is good: and
such faith is the reward and consolation, not the
product of old age.

Cicero refers to one other charge against old
age,—that the shadows of death are upon it, and

that the imminence of departure must perturb the last years of life. To this he replies that death ought to be regarded with perfect indifference if it completely annihilates the soul, or ought even to be desired if it leads forth into some region where it is destined to be immortal. This, however, is not a defence of age and its condition, but a recognition of the value of philosophy or faith in meeting the anxieties of age and overcoming the fear of death. As to regarding death with "perfect indifference", how can this be possible to a creature with any imagination? Oblivion or immortality! nothing or everything! If a man knew that instead of these tremendous alternatives he was destined within a few short years to be transplanted to some distant part of the earth to see his old home no more, this change, trivial in comparison with that of death, could not be a matter of indifference. The strange thing is that old people approach the stupendous event of death as calmly as they do.

Whatever views we may take as to the comparative powers, virtues, or satisfactions of youth and age, I believe that nothing but the spiritual force in man can redeem old age from degradation. As far as his physical nature is concerned it is obviously a degradation; his form and features become a travesty of what they were in his prime. He loses his teeth, his hair drops out or grows in the wrong places, his skin becomes wrinkled or his belly enlarged: he grows ugly. His debilitated organs subject him to a hundred maladies and discomforts. His intellectual powers also deteriorate, and nothing but a brave philosophy or a noble faith can save his moral nature from suffering also: without these the wisdom of the old is mere disillusion and their virtue the result of impotence. Gradually the senses which made him conscious of life become dulled; one by one the activities which made him a partner in life have to be relinquished. He who at one time knew that he was becoming *more* knows that he is becoming *less*. There was a time when he rejoiced daily in the conscious improvement of his faculties, now he has to watch their daily decline, and perhaps his greatest loss of all is his loss of the power to love life, which he may realise in his consciousness of that contrast between what he feels now and what he felt once, which comes to him in the sudden flashes of memory revived by the smell of a flower or the notes of an old song.

Love, it may be said, remains impregnable. For

the rising generation, for children and grandchildren, the old may feel a protective and unselfish love, which may meet with a generous
response; but when the old die no young heart is
broken; and between man and woman, husband
and wife, when old age comes the bond is just
comradeship. This comradeship may be strong
and beautiful, but it has nothing in common with
the passionate devotion, the ecstasy, which can
make love between a young man and woman the
greatest possession that Earth or Heaven could give.

We accept it as seemly that old age should
obey its limitations, we resent its simulations of
youth. The old man who marries a young woman
is the subject of ridicule, and January finds few
sympathisers when May is unfaithful. The old in
whom the lusts of the flesh outlive their virility,
are special objects of derision. They are thus described by Chaucer in the *Parson's Tale*:

These old dotards, yet wol they kisse, though they
may nought do. Certes, they been lyk to houndes; for
an hounde when he cometh by the roser or by other
busshes, though he may not pisse, yet wol he heve up
his leg and make a countenance to pisse.

We can, however, set no mark, make no definite
boundary between youth and age. The curve of

life is larger for one man than for another, and at the age of, say, sixty one may have completed his curve, while another may be but two-thirds of the way along his. January may sometimes be as efficient as October.

Whom the gods love die young. This saying has been interpreted in two ways. The first, the obvious reading, is that the gods wished to save the favoured from disillusion, and the discredit of old age and removed them at the zenith of their powers: the other reading is that those endowed with the finest spirit, the divinely inspired, whatever the length of their years never really do grow old, but preserve to the end a youthful and happy outlook. This is indeed the ideal of long life: for those whose courage, or love of their fellow creatures, or spiritual insight can triumph over their physical infirmities, the path of life instead of following the upward and downward curve, may be a continuous ascent until the end, its completion on some peak of vision.

It would seem as if the old,—and not only those of them who have definite religious convictions,— must have some unconscious faith that all is well, otherwise it is difficult to understand the placidity with which they live the few last years of their lives. If not extinction, at least a momentous change is imminent for them and we can hardly account for their calm by attributing it to mere stupidity or want of imagination. Unless they believe that their lives are linked with the permanent, every hour of those last years is a farewell.

> Dewdrops are the gems of morning
> But the tears of mournful eve,—

and every lovely thing of Earth, the flowers of Spring, the beauty of children, the bonds of love, must bring a pang of intense sadness to those who believe they are contemplating them for the last time. Those cheerful old people who enjoy their daily routine of life on the brink of the grave amaze me: they seem like Hardy's weather-beaten thrush singing on the dreary winter day, of whom he says

> Some blessed hope whereof he knew
> And I was unaware,

may have been its inspiration.

Some simple unconscious faith, such as the child has in life, the old may have in death.

Of old age itself I think nothing can be said in praise. It is a hardship, a trial, but like every other hardship it may strengthen the spirit that

163

meets it gallantly; indeed a man's fitness for any extension of life beyond the present would seem to be measurable by the fortitude of his soul in resisting the tyranny of time, and his intelligence in accepting its lessons.

Our first impression of life is a happy one, its first greeting to us is a welcome. But how different is the exit, the farewell! If the first words of life are sweet to Earth's children, the last ones are sorrowful. When the time to go hence has come and all that lies beyond is hidden, when we most need courage, we are reduced by sickness and pain to our lowest condition; we are incapable of appreciating anything that is beautiful and all life is darkened in our clouded vision.

It seems a discreditable exit; and the next change, the corruption of the body that once expressed the soul, is a shameful conclusion. So in our reading of life if we may find exhilaration and encouragement in the first impressions we receive, must we not set against that the discouragement and humiliation of the departure?

Of course if the purpose of Nature which gave us so kind a welcome is to get rid of us when our bodies are past work, though the method may not be gracious there may be kindness in the plan of making the guest so uncomfortable that he would wish to be gone, instead of turning him out when everything around him was most attractive. Our view as to this would depend on whether the guest were homeless, and turned out to die, or were a traveller who was on a journey which it was necessary for him to make.

If death be not a conclusion, if the transfer of the spirit from an outworn structure to a new one be a condition of continued life, then we may bid farewell with good cheer to that time-stricken body, and see in dissolution a necessary and beneficent process; but if there is no renewal, if extinction is the last act of the play, then we can only regard the death-bed and the grave as an anti-climax, a vile conclusion to a superb conception.

We have no proof that death is not the end; the evidence of our senses in the presence of a dead body tells us that death is the end; but there is an instinct within us that rejects this evidence, an innate faith in life which refuses to accept an ignoble betrayal of its promises.

We cannot define Life: Life is: it is known to us through its manifestations in natural organic structure. The force of life seems to be unceasingly seeking means of expression, seizing or embracing material, and building for itself temporary habitations, constructing with adaptation to surrounding conditions, here producing the flowering plant, here the winged insect, here the human form. The life-force acquires separate and individual existence in these structures, and can transmit the characteristics of the structures to descendants; but the individual structure has no self-contained cohesion or continuity, and when the life-force is withdrawn it suffers dissolution, and we say that it is dead.

It seems, indeed, a natural, inevitable process. We feel no shock, no regret that the flowers of last year have vanished, because we know that others like them will reappear. Their loss gives us no real sense of death such as we should have if the Spring returned without restoring its flowers, for that would mean that something in life itself was dead. It would seem reasonable that we should regard the human being, as we do the plant or bird, as a creature that perished with the dissolution of its bodily structure; but in the self-consciousness of the human being, something new, something different has claimed recognition. The self-conscious individual feels that he is not so

much the body through which the life-force is
expressed as a part of that force itself, and further,
—that he is less an expression of the life-force
than a presence that can contemplate and to some
extent direct and control that life-force,—a realisation which we may call his Spirit. Is, then, he
asks, this conscious Spirit the creator or creation
of his body? If it be its creation or emanation, he
has no life independent of the body: if it be the
creator, does it when the body suffers dissolution
find a new embodiment or manifestation?

The plain facts, the result of observation and
scientific inference from our knowledge, give no
encouragement to belief in the survival of the
personality beyond the duration of the structure
through which it found expression. A definite
event confronts us: one whom we know dies, is
committed to earth or fire, and ere long not even
a handful of ashes remains to tell of what was.
Nature indicates no process through which we can
picture the spirit we know finding re-embodiment;
observation shows us that certain characteristics
of the lost one may be perpetuated in his descendants: it is even conceivable that the very ego
he was conscious of may survive in his offspring;
but if so, he will be unconscious of the previous

existence and will thus have become another person. We change from one period of life to another, but memory gives continuity and coherence to the whole life. The only real survival of the individual would be one in which memory linked it with the previous life

It is such a renewal, a survival in which we should be connected with all we knew here, in which those we love and whose bodily forms we could recognise should be with us, that the human heart cries for, and of which, if he asks for proof, he will find none.

There can be no proof: with our limited capacities we cannot expect to learn the ultimate truth about life,—but we can seek for it nevertheless, and feel that we are at least taking the pathway that leads to truth.

The process of the life-force in its creation of structures from material elements is seen not only in plants and animals but in worlds. Systems with their suns, planets, and satellites are evolved by this creative process from the gases of the nebulae, and we must accept the conclusion of science that they will again fall to ruin and be dissipated. A time will come when the Earth will no longer be capable of life-expression,—or, in other words, life will have been withdrawn from it.

Is that expression of life which the Earth produced dead?

> In all the spheres it may be that the Earth
> Alone conceived and gave a wild rose birth;
> On Earth alone the swallow spread its wing,
> And nowhere else did any skylark sing,
> No pine tree caught the murmur of the seas,
> Nor white thorn gave its fragrance to the breeze.

> When the earth perishes at last, will all
> Her loveliness be gone beyond recall?
> Can life go on forever and forget ·
> Primrose and daffodil and violet?
> No soul escape from earth to tell the tale
> Of April woodlands and the nightingale?

All will be as though it never had been, utterly lost inasmuch as it has not been capable of reproduction, inasmuch as no life elsewhere has benefited by it,—unless,—unless the human spirit which saw and loved it is not extinguished by death,—unless in that deathless spirit the vanished years are treasured, the vanished home made permanent.

The nearest approach to *permanence* in life is seen in the self-conscious spirit which reflects and remembers: but for it there would be no record, no past. Changes are taking place continuously around us, and not only externally but within us, not only in our bodies but in our minds, in our characteristics, in our faiths. We seem hardly to be the same creature in childhood, in maturity, in old age, and yet we feel throughout that the conscious *I* is continuous and one: past, present, and to some extent future are linked in it.

Conservation of life through instincts of self-preservation and reproduction are in evidence throughout Nature. It looks as if she had made a further provision against death in the self-conscious spirit which can retain and recall scenes and persons which have no longer any visible existence. But this preservation in the spirit is also only temporary, a mere postponement and prolongation measurable by the duration of the sphere on which the life exists, unless the spirit itself survives its present embodiment.

This, if it be possible, would be a new evolutionary advance in the safeguarding and conserving of life. The human soul may be the guardian and treasurer of all the wonder and beauty of the Earth's passing day. Or should we rather say that the eternal treasury may be the spirit of God, of which man's spirit is a part?

We cannot conceive how the self-conscious personality may be re-manifested. Nature gives us no clue. We may imagine with Sir Oliver Lodge that there is an ethereal embodiment; we may say with the believer in God, "That is where God comes in"; but we are compelled to recognise this,—that only in the survival of the individual can all that we see passing away be preserved,— that if such a hope has a foundation in truth, we are in the midst of a living universe, and if not, of one which lives under perpetual sentence of death.

We put our faith in what we know, in what we have loved and have only been able to love through its material presentation.

We ought not to regard matter as gross, as a hindrance to the spirit, but as the instrument of the spirit's expression, and when inspired and shaped by the spirit as the most perfect work of creation. From the simplest plant to the forest tree, from the insect's wing to the plumage of the humming-bird, from the dewdrop on a rose, from the sunset on the ocean, to the light in human eyes, we see the artistry of creation.

Without the presence of the conscious and perceiving spirit all this material beauty has no existence; without the material reality the spirit has no home. We can look forward to no future existence that is not material, that will not show us the same manifestations of life that we know on Earth. The cry of our hearts for reunion with those we love is not for any shadowy or spiritual semblance of them, but for expression in a bodily presence which will represent them as fully as the earthly body. It is the soul's greatest longing and therefore we may hope that there is a reality which awakens that longing. If we cannot believe this, then rather than look forward to a rebirth in which all we know and love now would be forgotten, let us hope that we shall perish with our ideals.

If by death we mean not extinction but the dissolution of an outworn structure, this may be a necessary condition of the preservation of life. A continuous life of the body subject to the injuries, the wear and tear of time would be an unspeakable misfortune,—if indeed such a thing were possible: it would be an imprisonment of the spirit, its eternal punishment. For continued activity of the spirit there must be bodily renewal. If we try to picture the Earth or any limited sphere without death we are faced with the ridiculous; and if we try to picture a heaven of perfected immortals, revealed in some bodily guise which would not have been formed in response to necessities of nutrition and reproduction, we should also be faced with the ridiculous. We might indeed prefer annihilation to eternal domicile in such an asylum. The goal is but a stage on the quest, and life is for ever renewed in fulfilment.

This four-score years is as long a time as our temporal habitation can endure: the spirit may be willing but the flesh can hold it no longer: the navigation may be more efficient than ever, but the ship is leaking.

Pain is mortal. Suffering like every other evil has only to be severe enough and prolonged enough to result in death. Accepting our definition that the good is that which preserves, uplifts, and enlarges life and the evil that which degrades and destroys it, it follows that there can be no permanence of unhappy or evil conditions, as their prolongation leads to death. On the other hand there is no limitation to the possibilities of the life which has its creative impetus in goodness. The survival of the fittest which we see in Nature's

evolutionary processes, may also be the law of the
spiritual advance of creation.

Of such a progressive and continuous life we
have had an imaginative conception, and in our
bravest and best hours we have felt we can share
in it. I have often wondered whether life has
created any desires which are impossible of fulfilment,—whether, indeed, the desires are not evidence of the possibility of fulfilment. This is
shown in the activities of all the bodily functions,
but when we come to the aspirations of the self-
conscious spirit, we stand in doubt. In our hope
to live beyond our present limitations, has life
implanted in us desires which it cannot fulfil?
Why do we not regard death as an event as happy
and natural as birth? We have lived through our
allotted term of years, we have played our parts;
our bodies have known the pains and thrills of
being; they have grown worn and weary and ask
for rest. Why then should we desire any further
unrest, any breaking of the sleep? Is it because
our hope of the awakening is due to an inspiration within us that our present life is incomplete,
and that greater adventures await us?

Sleep after toyle, port after stormie seas,
Ease after warre, death after life does greatly please.

174

This expresses our attitude to our present life; but, mark! it is *port after stormie seas*, port, a home-coming, a pause, a haven of rest on the way,—not shipwreck, not a foundering with the loss of all hands, in an ocean that has no shores.

Let us then have faith in life and death! Let us believe that there is a great Heart of Life that cannot know defeat or death,—and that there is no aspiration, no love of which we are capable that is not a response to an eternal reality.

VIII

A READING OF POETRY

ACKNOWLEDGMENTS

Permission has been given by Messrs Longmans, Green & Co., and the Executrix of Miss Eva Gore-Booth, to quote "The Little Waves of Breffny"; by Messrs Sidgwick & Jackson, to quote Rupert Brooke's sonnet, "The Hill"; and by the late Mr. G. W. Russell (A. E.), to include his poem, "Two Magics". The author wishes to record his thanks for these privileges.

VIII

A READING OF POETRY [1]

THE emotion stirred by an intense realisation of life is the fountain-spring of poetry and the inspiration of art. It gives the incentive to celebrate and preserve in lasting form this experience; and it is significant that it chooses, or cannot help choosing, beautiful forms of expression, as though aware that only the beautiful is imperishable.

Of the various arts which poetry animates I will now speak only of that which is expressed through language. Sculpture, architecture, and painting have their medium provided for them in clay, stone, or pigment; music, except in its use of the human voice, has to construct its instruments; poetry finds its material in language, and this material varies more than the medium of any other art. Happy is the poet who has the heritage of a great language to work with, even as the architect is fortunate who has stone quarries and not brickfields at his command.

For its effect poetry depends more than any

[1] This essay has already been published as a separate volume.

other art on the percipient. Even the unimagina-
tive beholder can hardly fail to be impressed by
the majesty of such a building as St. Paul's Cathedral: the quarry is lifted into the heavens before
his eyes: his imagining is done for him. Even one
to whom music has no revelation may feel a stir-
ring of the pulses in listening to a chorus from
The Messiah; even one to whom no painting could
show "A light that never was on sea or land" may
appreciate the merits of a good picture; but poetry
is meaningless to him who has no poetry within
himself. However great may be the expression
which a poet gives to his vision, the essence of his
art is in suggestion, and his reader shares with
him the fulfilment of his work.

In the other arts, in architecture, sculpture,
painting, or music, the creative imagination is
more occupied with the medium in which it
works,—with form, or colour, or sound,—than
in poetry. In each of these arts there is a reading
of life, an interpretation of its beauty through a
special and limited medium, and the workmanship is of supreme importance; but in poetry the
conception is even more vital than the expression,
and its scope, which covers the whole range of
life, includes the creations of the other arts.

The process of time which has made the spirit
of man more complex has given to poetry a new
significance. It has become less the depiction or
celebration of the wonderful or beautiful things,
the joyful or tragic scenes which life exhibits, than
the interpretation of the joy and pain, the wonder
and beauty at the heart of life itself. It has become
less objective, more reflective, more conscious
than formerly of the bond between the human
spirit and the external world. Time has extended
the scope of poetry in this direction but has
limited it in another. Verse, the special structure
of poetry, was once the general vehicle of narrative, and in much of this narrative there was no
poetry. Now, prose romance or fiction does most
of the story-telling. When the singer was also the
narrator, poetry was the most popular of the arts,
but now it can look for no such adventitious
support. Narrative may be so illuminated by imagination as to become poetry: we then call it
Epic and recognise it in Homer and Virgil, Dante
and Milton. I do not say that a great narrative
poem is still an impossibility, but, to create it, a
poet must be born who can tell a story of new
adventure in which men can believe, as they once
believed in Olympus and Paradise and Tir n'an

oge, in the wanderings of Ulysses and the quest of the Holy Grail. Even in the narrative verse of the past there was much that hardly deserves the name of poetry. The *Aeneids*, with occasional beautiful passages, are full of prosaic matter, and *The Canterbury Tales* are just the merriest collection of stories in the English language. The insight of humour in reading life is akin to that of poetry; and the very poetry of laughter, or the laughter of poetry, rings out in some of Chaucer's descriptions of men and things; but apart from these interludes *The Canterbury Tales* would have lost little if they had been written in prose.

It is when the emotions are touched, that the fountain-springs of poetry well up, and we come upon these as oases in the dry expanses of much of the old heroic verse. In Homer himself it is only in rare lines or passages that the heart is moved. The rhythms of the greatest handler of the greatest of languages are a constant pleasure to the ear. We delight in the superb choice of words which give us such lines as:

ἕζετ᾽ ἔπειτ᾽ ἀπάνευθε νεῶν, μετὰ δ᾽ ἰὸν ἕηκεν·
δεινὴ δὲ κλαγγὴ γένετ᾽ ἀργυρέοιο βιοῖο,[1]

[1] There he sat apart from the ships and let an arrow fly, and terrible was the clanging of that silver bow.

in which we almost hear the clanging of Apollo's bow and the tremor of its string; but it is only rarely that Homer strikes the chords to which the deeper emotions of the heart respond,—as when, above the tumult of the wars of gods and men we are made to feel the pathos of human life and death in this passage:

ὣς φάτο, τοὺς δ' ἤδη κάτεχεν φυσίζοος αἶα
ἐν Λακεδαίμονι αὖθι, φίλῃ ἐν πατρίδι γαίῃ,

which has been thus beautifully translated by Dr. Hawtrey:

So said she; they long since in Earth's soft arms were reposing,
There in their own dear land, their fatherland Lacedemon.

It would be difficult to find in modern poetry more charming pictures than the *Odyssey* gives in such scenes as the home life of Nausicaa, or more delightful pastorals than the *Idylls* of Theocritus; but even in scenes of simple life, a deeper significance, a fuller response to their beauty has entered into modern poetry. Compare Theocritus and Keats.

The goatherd of Theocritus describes a carved bowl:

A deep bowl, too, of ivywood I will give thee, rubbed with sweet bees-wax, a twy-eared bowl newly wrought, smacking still of the knife of the graver. Round its upper edges goes the ivy winding, ivy besprent with golden flowers; and about it is a tendril twisted that joys in its saffron fruit. Within is designed a maiden, as fair a thing as the gods could fashion, arrayed in a sweeping robe and a snood on her head. Beside her two youths with fair love-locks are contending from either side with alternate speech, but her heart thereby is all untouched.[1]

And take a verse from the *Ode to a Grecian Urn*:

Heard melodies are sweet, but those unheard
  Are sweeter; therefore, ye soft pipes, play on;
Not to the sensual ear, but, more endear'd,
  Pipe to the spirit ditties of no tone:
Fair youth, beneath the trees, thou canst not leave
  Thy song, nor ever can those trees be bare;
Bold lover never, never canst thou kiss,
  Though winning near the goal—yet do not grieve;
She cannot fade though thou hast not thy bliss,
  Forever wilt thou love and she be fair.

In Theocritus we have just a beautiful description, in Keats something more: his is also

---

[1] Theocritus, *Idyll* i. A. Lang's translation.

a reading of the heart that contemplates the beauty and the truth that underlies it.

These views may seem to give too much importance to the value of the thought or emotion, too little to that of expression. It is true that fine workmanship may make attractive almost any theme, but equally so, that when the subject is trivial the poetry can never be great. On the other hand, however profound or beautiful the idea, unless it be expressed in beautiful form it is not poetry.

Poetry, as I said, demands, more than any art, a sympathetic response, and that response has innumerable variations. The colour and fragrance of a blossom depend not only on its seed, but on the nature of the soil in which it is sown. Even the poems that make the most universal appeal have different shades of meaning and subtleties of suggestion for different persons. Each of us must make his own anthology, and in the quotations I am giving in illustration of the reading of life through poetry, I am choosing those to which my own imagination has responded.

I believe that even for the child there is a

magic in the rhythm and choice of words. The
first picture I had of the wide world in winter was
held in the lines of a nursery rhyme:

> The North wind doth blow,
> And we shall have snow,
>   And what will the robin do then, poor thing?
> He'll sit in the barn,
> And keep himself warm,
>   And hide his head under his wing, poor thing!

The movement of the verse caught the mystery
of the sound of the wind in the growing darkness,
and gave a feeling of the protection of home,
which, with a child's sympathy with birds and
animals, was extended to the robin. And there
were two lines of a little hymn which, though as
simple as could be, opened enchanted pathways:

> There is a happy land
> Far, far away.

The rest of the hymn made no appeal,—it was
about saints and angels (who had none of the
attractions of fairies) but that line with the prolonged note,—"Far, far away", brought me my
first vision of regions beyond the world of every-
day life.

186

A READING OF POETRY

As a rule boys love romance and are un-
appreciative of poetry. Its deeper meanings are
not for the immature, though they may sometimes feel the fascination of its music. I remember how much I preferred to have my story
told in prose than in verse, how much better I
liked *Ivanhoe* and *The Talisman* than *Marmion* or *The
Lay of the Last Minstrel*; but in the midst of *The
Lady of the Lake* appeared a poem whose rhythm
gave enchantment to the whole scene that
evoked it:

> Soldier, rest! thy warfare o'er,
>   Sleep the sleep that knows not breaking;
> Dream of battled fields no more,
>   Days of danger, nights of waking.
>
> In our isle's enchanted hall,
>   Hands unseen thy couch are strewing,
> Fairy strains of music fall,
>   Every sense in slumber dewing.
>
> Soldier, rest! thy warfare o'er,
>   Dream of fighting-fields no more;
> Sleep the sleep that knows not breaking,
>   Morn of toil, nor night of waking.

The music of the verse gives the romantic scene

an abiding beauty, and its art,—unapparent
though unconsciously appreciated by the boy,—
is recognised by the critic in the change from
alternate rhymes in the first eight lines to couplets
in the last four.

The beauty of a single verse may open for
us pathways of romance that volumes of travel
records fail to discover:

> I remember the black wharves and the slips
>   And the sea tides tossing free:
> The Spanish sailors with bearded lips,
> And the beauty and mystery of the ships,
>   And the magic of the sea.

The enchantment of the Spanish Main and
seventeenth-century seas is revived in the spell of
those lines.

When poetry appeals to our boyhood it is either
in the opening of these paths into wonderland
or in the description of heroic deeds; and though
Macaulay can hardly be called a poet we remember

> How well Horatius kept the bridge
> In the brave days of old

and know that he could write poetry,—to say

which, however, is rather like the distinction made in Ireland between a man who is drunk and one who has "drink taken".

To boys, and perhaps to girls also, before sex begins to play upon their imaginations, love-poems are thoroughly distasteful; but to young men and women poetry becomes the exponent of love, and love the inspiration of poetry. And here poetry differs from the other arts: the lover feels the incentive to read, and even to write poems, but we do not find him impelled to make models in clay or architectural designs for a town hall. From the doggerel of a valentine to *The Song of Solomon* and the *Sonnets from the Portuguese*, verse has been the instrument of love.

The expansion which has taken place in the spirit of man, in his appreciation of beauty, his interpretation of Nature, his whole conception of the significance of life, is recorded in his poetry. In nothing is the process more marked than in his valuation of love. The poetry of the ancient world strikes no deep note of the wonder and beauty of love between man and woman. The amours of the gods, the fateful results of human passion, were themes of the classic poets of Greece and Rome; the old love-poems of Persia

189

and the East are exuberant expressions of the glamour of sex attraction. In them the love is neither interwoven with comradeship nor does it show any realisation of its influence as an ideal. Nevertheless in that poetry there was a recognition of the beauty of sex relationship which lifted it above mere physical desire. In the *Song of Songs which is Solomon's* there are verses which suggest a lovelier conception of a relationship than that of a voluptuary to a favourite concubine:

Rise up, my love, my fair one, and come away.
For, lo, the winter is past, the rain is over and gone;
The flowers appear on the earth;
The time of the singing of birds is come,
And the voice of the turtle is heard in our land;
  The fig tree putteth forth her green figs,
And the vines with the tender grape give a good smell.
  Arise, my love, my fair one, and come away.

    ·   ·   ·   ·   ·

My beloved is mine, and I am his.

Here the love of the woman is associated with the joy of the springtime and the beauty of life; —but this is exceptional. A more typical example of Oriental love is given by Omar Khayyám:

A READING OF POETRY

A book of verses underneath the bough,
A loaf of bread, a jug of wine, and thou
  Beside me singing in the wilderness,—
O wilderness were Paradise enow!

where we feel that the jug of wine was quite as
important as the lady.[1]

Much of the love-poetry of the world has been
rather superficial pretty stuff in praise of the
charms of the fair one, or in complaint about her
coldness. We feel that they are an expression of
love-making, not of love,—that if she proved
fickle no serious damage would have been done
to the heart of the lover. Poetry, which illu-
minates everything beautiful, has thrown its light
and shadow on the passing hours of these love
experiences and has given us exquisite lyrics in
their celebration:

Bid me to live, and I will live
  Thy protestant to be;
Or bid me love, and I will give
  A loving heart to thee.

⋅　　　⋅　　　⋅

[1] Hafiz, as the Aga Khan has recently reminded us, is a
finer poet than Omar Khayyám, but his love poems are
amorous rather than passionate, and show no understanding
of that bond of comradeship which gives love its deepest
meaning.

Bid me despair, and I'll despair
  Under that cypress tree;
Or bid me die, and I will dare
  Ev'n death to die for thee.[1]

But of course we know perfectly well that he didn't mean a word of it.

And what of this?—

Tell me not, sweet, I am unkind,
  That from the nunnery
Of thy chaste breast and quiet mind
  To war and arms I fly.

.   .   .   .

Yet this inconstancy is such
  As thou too shalt adore;
I could not love thee, dear, so much,
  Loved I not honour more.

In those last two lines poetry has given perfect expression to an ideal: the thought is here expressed once and for all time; but again we feel a moment's doubt as to whether a more ardent lover might not have felt "Loved I not honour *less*".

Dante treated love seriously, and Shakespeare

---

[1] Herrick, *To Anthea.*

knew how near its laughter is to tears; but it is
only in modern poetry that the full radiance of
its beauty, the pain of its failure, the immortality
of its hope, have been expressed. In no poems of
the past is the same intensity of emotion shown
as in those which have been written since the
beginning of the nineteenth century. Love in
these poems looks beyond its moments of realisation, it sees a beauty that asks for more than
the hours of our mortal life for fulfilment, it
recognises—

> Infinite passion and the pain
> Of finite hearts that yearn.

There is a note unheard in the past in such a
poem as this:

Breathless, we flung us on the windy hill,
  Laughed in the sun and kissed the lovely grass,
  You said, "Through glory and ecstasy we pass;
Wind, sun, and earth remain, the birds sing still,
When we are old, are old. . . ." "And when we die
  All's over that is ours; and life burns on
Through other lovers, other lips," said I,
  —"Heart of my heart, our heaven is now, is won!"
"We are Earth's best, that learnt her lesson here.

A READING OF LIFE

Life is our cry. We have kept the faith!'' we said;
  "We shall go down with unreluctant tread
Rose-crowned into the darkness!'' Proud we were,
And laughed, that had such brave true things to say.
—And then you suddenly cried and turned away.[1]

And was there ever a finer memorial of that
love between a man and woman where friendship
and love are one than this?

When you are old and I am passed away,—
Passed and your face, your golden face, is gray—
I think, whate'er the end, this dream of mine,
Comforting you, a friendly star will shine
Down the dim slope where still you stumble and stray.

So may it be: that so dead yesterday,
No sad-eyed ghost, but generous and gay,
May save you memories like almighty wine,
When you are old!

Dear Heart it shall be so. Under the sway
Of death the past's enormous disarray
Lies hushed and dark. Yet though there come no sign,
Live on well pleased: immortal and divine
Love shall still tend you as God's angels may
When you are old!

Of the work of poets who were contemporaries

---

[1] Rupert Brooke.

there has seldom been a greater contrast than between the rushing waves of Swinburne's love-rhapsodies and the quiet depth of Tennyson's more passionate poems. No poem of Swinburne has the intensity of *Oenone*, and in all literature it would be hard to find a more poignant cry of the heart's desire than that in *Maud* which suddenly follows the dark brooding of a troubled spirit:

> O that 'twere possible
> After long grief and pain,
> To find the arms of my true love
> Round me once again!

Nothing could be simpler, or, in its context more poignant.

And there is one modern poem, which though neither inspired by deep passion nor troubled by the ordeals and complexities of sex relations, stands almost alone in its perfection of expression of the freshness and delight of young love. The brightest beauty of sound and colour and fragrance is interwoven with the bridal song of *Love in the Valley*, so naturally that we hardly know whether we are being shown love revealed through beauty, or beauty illuminated by love:

> Sweeter unpossessed,
> Sweeter, for she is what my heart first awaking
> Whispered the world was; morning light is she.
> Love that so desires would fain keep her changeless,
> Fain would fling the net, and fain have her free.

As the old springs of romance,—the heroic war-fare, the conquest of the wild, the exploration of unknown shores,—have failed, the romance of the relation between the sexes has increased. Love is a far more important thing, a happier or a sadder thing, a greater danger and a greater inspiration than it was in the ancient world. Only in modern poetry do we find a comprehension of that union of comradeship with passion which can make the love between a man and a woman an inspiration and a lifelong faith. Those who may not be capable either of a great passion or a permanent loyalty must admit that this ideal bond may be realised, and have only to read such a poem as Browning's *By the Fireside* to rejoice in its beauty and recognise in its truth a mortal relationship which seems to have in it something that is deathless.

No less marked than the change in man's conception of love is his feeling about Nature. Some sympathetic bond with Nature must always have

existed in his heart, but the records we have show
that in the ancient world he saw her as something
outside his own life, and that the idea of a communion between her and his own spirit was un-
born. Flowers from time immemorial have stood
out in their fascination for man, — flowers and
stars,—but in the ancient world flowers had no
meaning for him beyond their own beauty. The
early Chinese poetry which is full of the love
of flowers never connects them with any deeper
emotion than a lover's passion or lament, or an
exile's memory of home; and in Oriental literature generally they bring with them the airs of
the gardens of pleasure, not any spiritual message:
roses and nightingales are part of the stage scenery
of a love-scene. All English literature is full of
the fragrance of flowers and the songs of birds,
more especially associated with the spring, with
the tidings of gladness and rebirth: they are em-
blems of the joy of life, but though Shakespeare
finds—

> Tongues in trees, books in the running brooks,
> Sermons in stones, and good in everything,

it was not until Wordsworth's day that the feeling
of communion between Nature and the spirit of

197

man found expression,—never before were heard such words as his—

> Thanks to the human heart by which we live,
> Thanks to its tenderness, its joys and fears,
> To me the meanest flower that blows can give
> Thoughts that do often lie too deep for tears.

To our forefathers it was enough that "melodious birds sang madrigals", or that "the lark at Heaven's gate sings", but in modern hearts the meaning of the songs as well as their melody brings a response: to Shelley, to Wordsworth, and to Meredith the lark's song came from the fountain-springs of life, and brought tidings of eternal beauty.

In *The Lark Ascending*, a lyric which comes nearer than any other I know to an expression of a voice in Nature, the sustained note of the bird is interwoven with the spirit of the listener:

> For singing till his heaven fills
> 'Tis love of Earth that he instils,
> And ever winging up and up,
> Our valley is his golden cup,
> And he the wine which overflows
> To lift us with him as he goes.

And one of the rare messages of hope which

the sombre spirit of Thomas Hardy received from
Nature came in the song of a bedraggled thrush
on a dreary winter day:

> So little cause for carollings
>   Of such ecstatic sound
> Was written on terrestrial things
>   Afar or nigh around,
> That I could think there trembled through
>   His happy good night air
> Some blessed Hope, whereof he knew
>   And I was unaware.

But then we ask, is there any meaning, any
message beyond that which the hearer gives: is he
not listening to the vibration of his own heart-
strings? The pure sweet notes of the robin which
W. H. Davies hears in his poem *Truth* had no
celestial source; they were notes of jubilation and
triumph caused by the fact that the bird has just
slain his father. And Meredith in his poem *Song
in the Songless* finds that the only music of the
sedges was within himself:

> They have no song, the sedges dry,
>   And still they sing.
> It is within my breast they sing
>   As I pass by.

Within my breast they touch a string,
  They wake a sigh.
There is but sound of sedges dry;
  In me they sing.

But there is still the wonder, "Within my heart
they touch a string". The most convincing imita-
tion of a natural sound by mechanical means, the
most perfect model of a flower could touch no
string in us, awake no sigh. With living things
we are drawn into comradeship, and even when
Nature may not make direct revelation to us she
becomes the instrument through which the spirit
finds utterance.

Love may be blind in its failure to see the
defects in the loved one, but no vision is so clear
as love's in reading the beauty. In this, the poetic
vision of life resembles the lover's, and its illumination of the beauty of reality shows us a
truth that abides when the illusions of its dreams
are forgotten. It is in this quality of imaginative
realisation that we receive through poetry a truer
conception of the full meaning of life than we get
from the reasonings of psychology.

It is not, however, when poetry sets out to

proclaim truth, not in didactic or philosophic poems that it gives us most light: not in the poems of Lucretius, or the *Essay on Man*, or the second part of *Faust*, or *The Excursion*, or *The Testament of Beauty*: it is in those flashes of insight, those whispers of unexpected beauty which touch the spirit and pass into music, the meanings held in brief passages,—it may be in a single verse or line,—that poetry enlarges the vision and reveals the human heart to itself. We are conscious of a clarifying of the vision in the significance which poetry can give to the simplest scene. Take, for example, Wordsworth's *Solitary Reaper*. Those moorland surroundings become to us a living reality, not in a description of their features, but in their relation to the human spirit.

> Will no one tell me what she sings?—
> Perhaps the plaintive numbers flow
> For old, unhappy, far-off things,
> And battles long ago.

The past transfigures the scene, and ancestral memories interpret it.

And what picture depicting in detail the charms of a fair lady in the manner of the sixteenth-century lyrics could give such a lovely portrait, as we have in the two lines:

> And beauty born of murmuring sound
> Shall pass into her face?

In *Stepping Westward* the poet again makes the touch of human sympathy the guiding light on the path of life, and interprets the unknown through the known:

> And while my eye
> Was fixed upon the glowing sky,
> The echo of the voice enwrought
> A human sweetness with the thought
> Of travelling through the world that lay
> Before me on my endless way.

In great poetry, in passages which thrill the imagination, the beauty of the thought and the music of the verse are perfectly wedded. There are lesser poems in which there is a beauty of rhythm and little meaning such as we find in much of Swinburne's verse; and there are others, —many of Wordsworth's for instance,—in which the art imperfectly embodies the conception. We have examples of perfect expression of the vision through the music in Milton. The dancing

trochees of *L'Allegro*, the rhymed iambics, with
the varied length of lines, in *Lycidas* are spontaneously attuned to their subjects; but it is in his
grander conceptions that the harmony of vision
and language is most marked. Familiar as are the
great passages in *Paradise Lost*, I cannot refrain
from quoting one of them in illustration:

> He scarce had ceas't when the superior Fiend
> Was moving toward the shore; his ponderous shield,
> Ethereal temper, massy, large and round,
> Behind him cast; the broad circumference
> Hung on his shoulders like the moon, whose Orb
> Through optic glass the Tuscan artist views
> At ev'ning from the top of Fesole,
> Or in Valdarno, to descry new Lands,
> Rivers or Mountains in her spotty Globe.
> His spear, to equal which the tallest Pine
> Hewn on Norwegian hills, to be the Mast
> Of some great Admiral, were but a Wand,
> He walkt with to support uneasie Steps
> Over the burning Marle, not like those steps
> On Heaven's Azure, and the torrid Clime
> Smote on him sore besides, vaulted with Fire;
> Nathless he so endur'd, till on the Beach
> Of that inflamed Sea, he stood and call'd
> His Legions, Angel Forms, who lay intrans't
> Thick as Autumnal Leaves that strow the Brooks
> In Vallombrosa, where th' Etrurian shades

High overarch't imbowr; or scattered Sedge
Afloat, when with fierce Winds Orion arm'd
Hath vext the Red-Sea Coast, whose waves o'er-
    threw
Busiris and his Memphian Chivalrie.

So we find in Tennyson a fairy scene made
real in elfin music:

> Only reapers, reaping early
> In among the bearded barley,
> Hear a song that echoes cheerly
> From the river winding clearly,
>   Down to towered Camelot:
> And by the moon the reaper weary,
> Piling sheaves in uplands airy,
> Listening, whispers "Tis the fairy
>   Lady of Shalott".

And it would be difficult to find a poem in
which the music and the picture are more con-
summately intermingled than in *The Lotus-Eaters*.
To quote one passage:

> There is sweet music here that softer falls
>   Than petals from blown roses on the grass,
> Or night dews on still waters between walls
>   Of shadowy granite in a gleaming pass;
> Music that gentlier on the spirit lies

Than tired eyelids upon tired eyes;
Music that brings sweet sleep down from the blissful
    skies.
Here are cool mosses deep,
And through the moss the ivies creep,
And in the stream the long-leaved flowers weep,
And from the craggy ledge the poppy hangs in sleep.

In these last lovely lines an echo comes from
far away, for did not Virgil write—

Muscosi fontes et somno mollior herba.

It is by virtue of the qualities of those poems,
or passages from poems which form but a small
proportion of the bulk of their work, that even
the great poets win their immortality. This is so
obvious that I need give no examples, for even in
a poet who was so seldom uninspired as Keats,
it is through the odes, and sonnets, and a few
passages in his longer poems that he takes his
high place. In the odes the beauty of expression
has never been excelled, and there are lines in
Hyperion which have a movement as fine as Milton's, such as these in which we hear the passage
of the wave of wind across the silent forest at
night:

As when upon a tranced summer night,
Those green-robed senators of ancient woods,
Tall oaks, branch-charmed by the earnest stars,
Dream, and so dream all night without a stir,
Save from one gradual solitary gust
Which comes upon the silence, and dies off,
As if the ebbing air had but one wave;—
So came these words and went.

Shelley spun acres of poetic gossamer, but seldom gave us a revelation. His emotions are too excited, their expression lacks restraint. Occasionally, as in the *Ode to the West Wind*, there is a roll of deep harmonies and in *Prometheus Unbound* there are some great passages, and lovely whispers of fairy music, as in the lines—

A wind arose among the pines; it shook
The clinging music from their boughs, and then
Low sweet faint sounds, like the farewells of ghosts
Were heard: Oh follow, follow, follow me——;

but his art seldom gives substance to his conception. In one of his most beautiful poems, the ode *To a Skylark*, the verse form fails to suggest the unbroken flow of the bird's notes:

Hail to thee, blithe spirit!
Bird thou never wert—

That from Heaven or near it
   Pourest thy full heart
In profuse strains of unpremeditated art.

The ponderous Alexandrine of the final line
checks the joyful music of the song which is
perfectly expressed in Meredith's verses:

He rises and begins to round,
He drops the silver chain of sound,
In many links without a break,
In chirrup, whistle, slur and shake,
All intervolved and spreading wide,
Like water-dimples down a tide
Where ripple ripple overcurls
And eddy into eddy whirls;
A press of hurried notes which run
So fleet they scarce seem more than one.

Both poets in listening to the glad notes of the
bird breathe the same sigh of regret in contrasting
them with the outpourings of the human heart.
So Shelley says:

We look before and after,
   We pine for what is not:
Our sincerest laughter
   With some pain is fraught;
Our sweetest songs are those that tell of saddest
   thought.

And Meredith:

> Was never voice of ours could say
> Our inmost in the sweetest way,
> Like yonder voice aloft, and link
> All hearers in the song they drink.

The recognition of the relationship between the simple phenomena of Nature and the complexities of the human spirit is here again seen as a characteristic of modern poetry.

Much of Browning's work, the greater part of his longer poems, would have been more fittingly written in prose than verse: it is mere talking; but when he does sing it is to new and haunting musical movements. No poem in the language has the same rhythmical effect, none is more beautiful than this which begins:

> Where the quiet-coloured end of evening smiles
>   Miles and miles
> On the solitary pastures where our sheep
>   Half asleep
> Tinkle homeward through the twilight. . . .

It is so original, so entirely Browning's own, that no other poet has ventured to copy it. He has also discovered the effect that can be won from the artistic use of colloquial language:

through it he gives a homely charm to profound or passionate themes. In *By the Fireside* the fervours of love, the sublimity of a mountain scene, the whole mystery of the relationship between soul and soul, gain rather than lose intensity when recalled in the shelter of the hearth. The note of that interpretation is struck in the familiarity of the first words of the poem:

> How well I know what I mean to do
> When the long dark autumn evenings come,

and throughout this, as in other poems of his, we are made to feel that there is nothing too solemn or sublime to be linked with the intimacy of daily life, and nothing too common in life to have an eternal significance. He and Wordsworth have shown that it is often by the most familiar paths that we reach the deepest mysteries of the spirit.

So closely are truth and beauty related that the music of rhythm loses its charm when the conception it expresses is unreal or not beautiful. Swinburne's metrical feats are often comparable to the rattle of notes on the keyboard of an instrument to which no strings respond. The sound of falling water may be the same if it comes from the discharge of a pumping station as over the rocks of a mountain stream, but what a difference in the music the spirit would hear! The fine rhythm of *Dolores* becomes a mechanical outflow of words for lack of inspiration in the poem. Take such a verse as this:

> By the ravenous teeth that have smitten
>> Through the kisses that blossom and bud,
> By the lips intertwisted and bitten
>> Till the foam has a savour of blood,
> By the pulse as it rises and falters,
>> By the hands as they slacken and strain,
> I adjure thee, respond from thine altars,
>> Our lady of pain—

which is a cataract of sound, signifying nothing. Compare with this the verse of a chorus in *Atlanta*, where the conception is lovely and the verse expresses it with perfect art:

> Where shall we find her, how shall we sing to her,
>> Fold our hands round her knees and cling?
> Oh that man's heart were as fire that could spring to her,
>> Fire or the strength of the streams that spring!
> For the stars and the winds are unto her
>> As raiment, as songs of the harp-player;
> For the risen stars and the fallen cling to her,
>> And the south-west wind and the west wind sing.

Or compare:

> The high gods took in hand
>   Fire and the falling of tears
> And a measure of sliding sand
>   From under the feet of the years—

a grand swinging metre, which is here stultified
because it expresses nonsense, with such lines as
these from *The Deserted Garden*:

> The fields fall southward, abrupt and broken,
>   To the low last edge of the long lone land—

where the beauty of the picture and the loveliness of sound become one.

Those lines in *The Solitary Reaper*—

> Perhaps the plaintive numbers flow
> For old unhappy far-off things,
>   And battles long ago—

have a quality hard to define, which Matthew
Arnold called "natural magic". It touches a note
of mystery which becomes an interpretation of
the actual,—it transports us to a wonderland that
seems more real than the place in which we were.
Matthew Arnold held that this quality has its
source in the Celtic imagination and was the

essential characteristic of Celtic poetry, though he finds some of his chief examples in other directions, quoting Keats's

> Magic casements opening on the foam
> Of perilous seas in faerylands forlorn

as a typical instance. We need not look far for others: we find them in the verses I have already quoted from *The Lady of Shalott*, and in those from *Hyperion* and *Prometheus Unbound*. In *The Ancient Mariner* and *Kubla Khan*, in many of Blake's poems the same spell is woven, and Matthew Arnold finds it constantly in Shakespeare, giving this passage from *The Merchant of Venice* in illustration:

> The moon shines bright . . .
> . . . in such a night
> Stood Dido with a willow in her hand
> Upon the wild sea-banks, and waved her love
> To come again to Carthage.

That this quality is the dominant note of Celtic poetry I think there can be no question. In our Irish poetry the imagination has always been greater than the power of expression,—the conception being often too glamorous to allow of embodiment,—but, where the note of wonder has been caught in the music, we have been given exquisite poetry. It appears alike in the old and the new. Here are some verses from an old West of Ireland ballad translated by Lady Gregory:

O Donall og, if you go across the sea, bring myself
    with you and do not forget it; and you will have
    a sweetheart for fair days and market days, and
    the daughter of the King of Greece beside you at
    night.

    .   .   .   .   .

When I go by myself to the Well of Loneliness, I
    sit down and I go through my trouble; when I see
    the world and do not see my boy, he that has
    an amber shade in his hair.

    .   .   .   .   .

You have taken the east from me; you have taken the
    west from me; you have taken what is before me
    and what is behind me; you have taken the moon,
    you have taken the sun from me; and my fear is
    great that you have taken God from me.

In modern Irish poetry the old glamour persists as its chief characteristic. In spite of the desecrations of the Earth's Sanctuaries by mechanical progress, in the tumult of the city street, everywhere, our modern Irish poets—pre-eminently W. B. Yeats, A. E. and James Stephens—find

gateways into fairyland. Here is one of the latest
poems of A. E.:

Have they the same enchantment, these children
    straying
In streets where electric moonlight and scintillating
    rose
Shed blooms on the ashen air, as those other children
Crouched in trance under hedgerows where hawthorn
    thickens its snows;

Or those others, who under a real moon and stars
Move to deeper wonder in themselves, who are still,
Who touch each other but gently, lest they break the
    magic
That makes them one with it on the night-shadowy
    hill.

Mr. Yeats's work is happily too well known for
it to be necessary to give examples, but I may
quote one poem from another Irish poet, Eva
Gore-Booth, in lovely illustration of this spell
which words can weave:

The grand road from the mountain goes shining to the
    sea
And there is traffic in it, and many a horse and cart,
But the little roads of Cloonagh are dearer far to me,
    And the little roads of Cloonagh go rambling
      through my heart.

A great storm from the ocean goes shouting o'er the hill,
  And there is glory in it, and terror in the wind,
But the haunted air of twilight is very strange and still,
  And the little winds of twilight are dearer to my
    mind.

The great waves of the Atlantic sweep storming on
    their way,
  Shining green and silver with the hidden herring
    shoal,
But the little waves of Breffny have drenched my
    heart in spray,
  But the little waves of Breffny go stumbling through
    my soul.

In English poetry subtleties of suggestion in
rhythm, though occasionally found in the older
poets, are a modern development. In Greek and
Latin verse though the hexameter was pre-
eminent, there was considerable metrical variety.
I must leave it to better qualified scholars to
say whether in these there were refinements
of rhythmical effect comparable to those I have
instanced in English. English verse has found its
surest foundation, and also its imprisonment, in
iambic verse, and for nearly a century it flowed
less like a river than a canal between the banks
of the heroic couplet. Blake broke the monotony,

but it was not until the nineteenth century that the new possibilities of music in verse were realised. One after another, Coleridge, Shelley, Keats, Tennyson, Swinburne, Browning, Meredith, Henley, and Stevenson, were discoverers in rhythm, and Yeats is of the same great company.

In considering poetry in its vision and reading of life I think it may be said that its truest readings are expressed in its finest music. The readings may vary from interpretations of life's deepest and saddest emotions to its lightest and gayest, but the verse is always appropriate. You may test it by comparing the accepted fine passages in any great poet with the forgotten ones. Wordsworth, whose voice when writing about domestic trivialities was "the bleat of an old sheep", rolled out great harmonies when his conception was a great one. His sonnet *"The world is too much with us"* is charged with emotional thought which flows with solemn grandeur to the full volume of the last lines:

Great God I had rather be
A pagan suckled in a creed outworn;
So might I, standing on this pleasant lea,
Have glimpses that would make me less forlorn;
Have sight of Proteus rising from the sea,
Or hear old Triton blow his wreathéd horn.

And it is interesting to notice here the value which a line or phrase gathers from its position in the structure of a verse, and also how much it may gain or lose by the smallest alteration in the words or their arrangement. In Spenser's *Colin Clout's come home again* occurs a line which differs only in one word from the last line in Wordsworth's sonnet. Spenser says:

> Of them the shepherd that hath charge in chief
> Is Triton blowing loud his wreathed horn.

Though the words are almost identical (it was a daring "crib"), the context, the subject, and the position of the line in the structure of the poem give Wordsworth's a force and a music which are absent in Spenser's.

Some artistic inspiration seems to guide the poet to the fitting rhythmical form in which to express his conception. We could not think of *The Ancient Mariner* as written in any other than the simple ballad verse in which we have it:

> He holds him with his skinny hand:
> There was a ship! quoth he.
> Hold off! unhand me, grey-beard loon!
> Eftsoones his hand dropped he.

No other metre would have compelled us, like

the wedding guest, to such spell-bound attention.
The twilight peace, the reverie, of Gray's *Elegy*
is perfectly conveyed in its verse; the dream of
The Lotus-Eaters and the lazy lift of the ocean
swell in the movement of the lines of that poem;
the revolutions of the engine, the purr of the
dynamos in the reverberating beats of the rhythm
in *McAndrew's Hymn.* I could give a hundred
instances of this accord in true poetry between
matter and manner, and I will cite one more example, Stevenson's *"Home no more home to me"*,
which seems to hold in its cadence the essence
of its subject, the pathos of farewell:

Spring shall come, come again calling up the wildfowl,
   Spring shall bring the sun and rain, bring the bees
     and flowers;
Red shall the heather bloom over hill and valley,
   Soft flow the stream through the even-flowing hours:
Fair the day shine as it shone on my childhood—
   Fair shine the day on the house with open door:
Birds come and cry there and twitter in the chimney—
   But I go forever and come again no more.

Perhaps this poem may have a special charm for
me because of its associations. When I was a
young man I paid a very happy visit to Stevenson

in Samoa, and he read me this poem which was
then unpublished; and now I can never read it
without recalling the tone of his voice and the
beauty which it gained by his prolongation of
certain accents in the rhythm, which I particu-
larly remember in the line

The *kind* hearts, the *true* hearts that loved the place of
   old.

He told me that he considered the capture of
rhythmical effect to be one of the greatest adventures of a poet. He said he was always hoping to
achieve it, often in vain (we have only to read
his *Songs of Travel* to see his successes), and he
instanced Yeats as the modern poet whose music
had carried us farthest into undiscovered regions.
He cited *The Lake Isle of Innisfree*, a poem much
less familiar in 1893 than it is to-day, as an
illustration; and so assured did I feel of the
enchantment of the music in its verse, that I was
amazed to find that George Meredith, to whom
I afterwards introduced this poem, found in it no
charm, and said that the writer did not respect
the difference between short and long. This seems
the more remarkable when we remember that
some of Meredith's loveliest rhythmical effects

219   P

are won from unexpected variations, as in many
of the lines of *Love in the Valley* and *The Day of the
Daughter of Hades*. But perhaps Meredith's variations are always *within* the structure of his poem's
chosen rhythm; he kept within bounds which he
considered Yeats to have broken. Henley was
another brave and successful adventurer in metrical
movement, and for this alone he deserves a high
place among English poets. His volumes *Rhymes
and Rhythms* and *The London Voluntaries*, are full of
the music of original movements; and let me
quote one of his poems as an instance of the
beauty that can be expressed in what is called
vers libre, and as a contrast to the pieces of prose
cut into irregular lines which most of the practitioners of this form of poetry offer to us:

> A late lark twitters from the quiet skies;
> And from the West,
> Where the Sun, his day's work ended,
> Lingers as in content,
> There falls on the old grey city
> An influence luminous and serene,
> A shining peace.
>
> The smoke ascends
> In a rosy-and-golden haze. The spires
> Shine and are changed. In the valley

A READING OF POETRY

Shadows rise. The lark sings on. The sun,
Closing his benediction,
Sinks, and the darkening air
Thrills with a sense of the triumphing night—
Night with her train of stars,
And her great gift of sleep.

So be my passing!
My task accomplished and the long day done,
My wages taken and in my heart
Some late lark singing,
Let me be gathered to the quiet west,
The sundown splendid and serene
Death.

New rhythmical movements give us the thrill
of discovery, not the shock of intrusion; but
nothing ever really surprises us if it be beautiful:
we seem to have expected it.

With some few exceptional cases, we see that
there is a relationship between the music and
the thought in poetry. We find the graceful six-
teenth- and seventeenth-century love-courtesies
singing to the tune of a madrigal, and the greater
and graver passages of poetry sounding in sonorous
harmonies. The theme is not deliberately fitted to
a musical measure: the music is controlled by the

theme. In the greater part of the verse of the eighteenth century there was little music, and in its subjects there was little to demand music. Pope was less a poet than a brilliant essayist who wrote in rhyme. Here and there the iambic couplets and quatrains of this period flowed with a sedate beauty like a river between grassy banks, as in the verse of Gray and Goldsmith—and in both these poets their music was a true expression of their themes; but the whole of that century was almost songless, because it held a commonplace and pedantic view of life.

I can hardly recall an instance in poetry where a great conception, an inspiring thought, a beautiful scene has been made real to us in verse which is not in itself beautiful; and but few of verse that gives a sense of its beauty where its theme was uninspiring.

We have illustrations of the dependence of poetry on the union between conception and expression in the effect of translation, which can only rarely do justice to its original. Greek is so glorious a language that it must have been created by a race which was inspired by beauty. French, for all its clarity, and its delicacy in the expression of wit, is so prosaic and un-musical that

we can hardly be surprised that France has produced no great poets. Homer owes more than any
other poet to the language in which he sang.
Every Greek scholar would place his poetry above
that of the Hebrew prophets; but (though I do
not forget the enthusiasm of Keats) I think a
reader unacquainted with Greek or Hebrew would
see finer poetry in the Book of Job, and the
prophet Isaiah, as presented in the authorised
English version of the Bible, than in the con-
temporary verse of Chapman's translation of
Homer. Though I am convinced that great verse
is inspired by great conceptions, I must admit
that there are exceptions, of which Homer is
an illustration, where the verse may be great in
itself.

Since writing the preceding part of this essay
I have had the pleasure of reading Mr. A. E.
Housman's delightful lecture, "The Name and
Nature of Poetry". I find much that he says in it
illuminative but I cannot agree with his main
contention. "Poetry", he declares, "is not the
thing said, but a way of saying it." I believe it is
equally the thing said and the way of saying it,
and that it is generally the beauty of the thought

that creates the beauty of the expression. He
quotes Shakespeare's

> Take, O, take those lips away,
> That so sweetly were forsworn—

which he says is nonsense but ravishing poetry.
It is neither: it expresses charmingly one of the
lighter moods of love. And though the quotations he gives from Blake have the same sort of
enchantment as a landscape seen in a mist, I am
unable to regard them as great poetry. He values
too highly the lightning-flash of madness—the
product of the emotional storm in the unbalanced
intellect. But there is nothing so sane as genius,
and the great poets read life not in the flash of
tempest but in the steady light of day or the calm
and constant mystery of starlight.

If the picture brought to the mind by the
words of the poem be not beautiful, the words
themselves convey little beauty. Take an instance
which I have already quoted of rhythmical charm:

> Where the quiet-coloured end of evening smiles
>   Miles on miles
> On the solitary pastures where the sheep
>   Half asleep . . .

from *Love among the Ruins*, and compare it with
another very similar measure:

> When the coster's done a-jumping on his mother,
>   On his mother—

which *is* nonsense but not ravishing poetry. We
then see how much the effect of the expression
depends on the *quality* of the thing said.

Whether or not we can accept Mr. Housman's
reading of poetry we find in it a refreshing robust-
ness. He has a sense of beauty in verse which he
does not attempt to subject to analysis. In marked
contrast to his broad appreciation is the anatomical
criticism of Miss Edith Sitwell, who in her
Pleasures of Poetry comes to her subject provided
with a foot-rule and a tuning-fork. The verse of
great poets which flowed spontaneously from their
conceptions is treated by her as though its rhythms
had been a matter of deliberate calculation.
Numerical values are given to the syllables and
the words ticketed. Here is an instance of her
treatment of a line of Swinburne's

> 2   6   6¾   6 4   2
> Red summer burns to the utmost ember.

when the sounds are priced like cheap articles of
clothing in a ladies' shop.

Mr. Housman's ear for the music in poetry is natural and true: he relies on it and asks for no scientific test. Miss Sitwell's ear is unreliable, her tests are mechanical, and she is more concerned in making her own marks on the score than in listening to the music.

Discussion as to the relative importance of subject and manner in poetry is no new one. The older Greek view was didactic: so was the Hebrew. S. H. Butcher in his commentary on Aristotle's *Poetics* finds in this treatise the first attempt to separate the theory of aesthetics from that of morals. Aristotle, he says, maintains that the end of poetry is a refined pleasure, and that if the poet fails to produce the proper pleasure he fails in the specific function of his art: he may be good as a teacher but as a poet or an artist he is bad. We can readily agree with Aristotle's ruling, but is not the converse equally true? May we not say that if the poet is bad as a teacher,— that is, if his reading of life is a feeble or untrue one,—he will fail to give the proper pleasure, and, consequently, as a poet be bad? The poet must be both a seer and an artist.

Butcher goes on to quote Sir Philip Sidney,

who in his *Apologie for Poetrie* repeatedly states
that the end of poetry is "delightful teaching",
or "to teach and delight". The word "teaching"
has too restricted a meaning for application here;
but if by "teaching" we may understand not
mere intellectual enlightenment or moral eleva-
tion, but an illuminative reading of life in all
its aspects, we may accept Sir Philip Sidney's
definition.

We are brought back to the definition with
which we started: Poetry is the expression of the
emotion caused by an intense realisation of life.
The record of the experience does not give delight
unless it be adequately and beautifully expressed,
and not until then does it become poetry. I
maintain that in Poetry the thing said and the
way of saying it are interdependent, and that the
greater conceptions inspire the finer forms of
expression.

New rhythmical beauty is born of new emotional inspiration. We have abundant evidence
of the horrible results when a deliberate attempt
is made at originality of form and there is no
inspiration. In the affairs of men there are times
when abuses or stagnations lead to rebellion, and
literature, as well as politics and religion, has been

strengthened by these reactions. In recent times we have had some revolt against tradition in poetic expression which offers us no new beauty of form, but merely an alternative of eccentricity and ugliness. The *vers libre* has degenerated into affectation or incoherence. The latest examples have no sort of structure,—lines of prose, and very bad prose, are divided in haphazard fashion and are offered as a substitute for rhythm—poverty of inspiration disguised in incoherence.

Among the writers who have played the fool with our language I hardly like to include Mr. Ezra Pound, as he has shown himself capable of skilful workmanship; but he has misused his strength and has become a contortionist. Mr. T. S. Eliot (who despises Milton) has never written a beautiful or fine line. His notoriety is probably founded on his obscurity. He has concealed commonplace thoughts behind a network of incoherent language which his applauders have mistaken for a veil hiding profundities. He and writers of his school find their audience among those who have formed no standard from knowledge of the great literature of the past, and who above all things wish to be thought modern in their views. Miss Sitwell and Mr. Sacheverell

Sitwell[1] are self-conscious strugglers after originality, and are often deliberate posers. Miss Gertrude Stein is, of course, a pure humbug. And God help those who mistake the eruptive cacophany of Mr. James Joyce for poetry.

Here is a specimen of the quality of this school of writers:

The wire-like bands of colour involute mount from
     my fingers;
  I have wrapped the wind round your shoulders
  And the molten metal of your shoulders bends into
     the turn of the wind,
AOI!
  The whirling tissue of light
    is woven and grows solid beneath us;
  The sea-clear sapphire of air, the sea-dark clarity,
    stretches both sea-cliff and ocean.[2]

But this, though uncouth mouthing, cannot compete in imbecility with the following:

> They say the lion and
> but here lizards life-flashes

---

[1] Miss Sitwell should bring her tuning-fork to the correction of her brother's ear. More than once he makes *balms* rhyme with *arms*.

[2] Ezra Pound, *Selected Poems*.

A READING OF LIFE

Over stormy rocks why
do the english hate life
but so does raucous italy
fingering cento lire
        but
that oleander mouth is
diverse spirit wavering
        in agate eyes
the inner fire consumes
        and life renews.[1]

Vers libre in itself can be welcomed, but it must be true to its name and show the liberty of strength, not the insubordination of weakness. It may then be the herald of new harmonies in poetry. The limited number of words that rhyme in the English language is a restriction to originality in verse, and as the volume of production increases the difficulty is emphasised. There are numerous words with which only one or two others rhyme, and we have but to see such a word as "furled" at the end of a line to know that we are about to be confronted with "world". As Milton foreshadowed, it looks as though we should have to make ourselves independent of rhyme for our music in verse and trust wholly to

[1] Richard Aldington.

rhythm.[1] Here the *vers libre* departure is a promising adventure: it may lead to the discovery of larger and more intricate rhythmical movements than those of the accepted measures. There may be flood-tides of emotion whose expression may triumphantly sweep over established barriers and find new channels; and then there will be power and rhythm in the movement. But the examples we are generally given lack all spontaneity: there is no flow, and the freedom claimed is exhibited in spasms and jerks. These poets cannot soar; their flight reminds us of the efforts of the plucked parrot that flapped its naked wings and said "Damme I *will* fly".

Henley seems to me to have shown more successfully than any other poet that the new freedom can produce new music, and I recommend a study of his work to our younger poets.

D. H. Lawrence, who lived in constant slavery of his emotions, was always proclaiming his freedom. Whatever may be thought of him as a psychologist of the morbid, he was a bad poet. He was one whose "little twist of brain" led to a misreading of life, to the vision of "a beauteous

[1] As in the poetry in the Irish language the use of assonances may be greatly developed.

231

face in a cracked glass". His thoughts would not *sing*, but, unlike the writers just referred to, he was earnest in his efforts to find expression for what he felt. Among them all we find an unhealthy self-consciousness. Their morbid introspection has been belauded as interpretation of subtle human emotion; but in most cases the self-revelation would be better described as indecent exposure. Of the sort of stuff they produce I will give no further quotations. If such writers have any vision, it is of life in its most disagreeable aspects, and they express this in the decomposition of language.

We cannot be too critical in our examination of what is called obscurity in poetry,—in our discrimination between a difficulty in reading the meaning which may be due to profundity or mysticism in the conception, and that which is due to bad workmanship.

The obscurity which has no excuse can be traced to four sources:

The fumblings of a confused mind among its own sensations.

Ignorance of the value of the language used, and of its syntax and prosody.

Deliberate distortion of that language, with the object of producing an original effect, or of giving an impression of profundity to commonplace thoughts.

The introduction of abstruse allusions, or remote historical references which convey no meaning to those who are not specialists in certain subjects.

The first three of these forms of obscurity are to be found in the incoherent *vers libres* to which I have referred. Of the fourth, even great poets have been guilty, and among them is Browning, who assumes in some of his longer poems that the reader is familiar with the family histories of mediaeval Italy. Such devices introduce the irritation of the cross-word puzzle into poetry.

But there is another sort of obscurity, or rather difficulty, in poetry which is essential in the conception and is, indeed, inevitable. Ideas which are already familiar to the mind, emotions which the heart has fully realised can be expressed in clear and definite language; but there are ideas not yet fully grasped by the mind, truths of which we have only premonitions. The expression of these in language can at first be only indefinite;

they must be approached by suggestion, by imaginative illustration. They demand imagination on the part of the reader, and their obscurity or lucidity will vary with the imagination that receives them. The indefiniteness which is found in some of our mystic poets, such as Blake or George Russell (A. E.), and in many of the poems of Browning, Meredith, and Yeats, is not obscurity, but the first light that shines on obscure regions.

Beauty may be defined as a manifestation through the senses of the essential goodness of life. Filtered through human thought, warmed by human emotion, this beauty finds expression in poetry. It may be asked whether poetry cannot have evil as its theme, and the answer is that it can have it as its theme but not as its inspiration. In the very power of the poetic imagination to make us realise the ugliness of evil it becomes a protest against evil. We must not confuse roughness or crudity with ugliness, and in poetic forms there may be a certain coarseness of outline, a lack of finish in detail which cannot be so described, —which indeed may be a true expression of certain bold conceptions. We find this in the work of Walt Whitman. His inspiration is plebeian

234

humanity, especially American humanity, and the growing-pains of a new world, and his verse moves like an undrilled mob, but his message is sincere and he expresses it at times with a rugged beauty. There is a greatness about Whitman's crudities: in ugliness there is always meanness and this is apparent in those desecrations of poetic art which I have quoted.

Ugliness is obvious, we turn away from it, but poetry has a more insidious danger to meet in the counterfeit of beauty,—the sentimentality of superficial emotion, "prettyness" or "precious-ness" of expression. I do not refer to the masses of verse, from the drawing-room song to the sportsman's doggerel which is popular with people who avoid poetry, just as trivial airs from light opera or negro hymns and dances may be pleasing to those who are deaf to music; but there is a danger of conventional diction and artificiality adulterating the work even of true poets. To take but one instance: Tennyson, great artist as he was, has done much to belittle his reputation by pre-senting the scenes of the great Arthurian legend in the atmosphere of the ladies' school and the Deanery, and by the insipidity and the prettyness of the blank verse in which these and his domestic

Idylls are written. No doubt it is a reaction against the conventional and stereotyped in poetry that evokes much of the rebellious ugliness I have deplored; but the antidote against all poetic adulteration is not the ugliness of deformity but the severity of truth.

That intense realisation of life which I have suggested as the fountain-spring of poetry is accompanied by unusual keenness and truthfulness of observation. Observation is the basis of science: science sees, but poetry often foresees, and at times poetry and science meet on the borderland of discovery. Keenness of observation in detail is always appearing in poetry. Who but Shakespeare made us look for the cinque-spotted drops in the bottom of a cowslip? Who but Virgil made us hear so clearly the sound of a galloping horse? Coupled with this keenness of observation the poet instinctively chooses from a mass of details the essentials which stand out and illuminate the whole picture. We might look almost at haphazard through the work of great poets and find illustrations. To take an example or two,—the first I can think of—what a perfect picture, and with what economy of detail, we have of hard winter, winter as we know it still but with a

flavour of the past preserved, in this song from
Love's Labour's Lost:

> When icicles hang by the wall,
>   And Dick the Shepherd blows his nail,
> And Tom bears logs into the hall,
>   And milk comes frozen home in pail,
> When blood is nipped, and ways be foul,
> Then nightly sings the staring owl,
>   Tu-Whit!
> Tu-Who! a merry note,
> While greasy Joan doth keel the pot.
>
> When all aloud the wind doth blow,
>   And coughing drowns the parson's saw,
> And birds sit brooding in the snow,
>   And Marian's nose looks red and raw,
> When roasted crabs hiss in the bowl,
> Then nightly sings the staring owl,
>   Tu-Whit!
> Tu-Who! a merry note,
> While greasy Joan doth keel the pot.

And here is a verse where the accuracy of observation and the choice of detail make the picture
memorable:

> With blackest moss the flower-plots
>   Were thickly crusted, one and all;

237

The rusted nails fell from the knots
  That held the pear to the gable-wall,
The broken sheds looked sad and strange;
  Unlifted was the clinking latch;
  Weeded and worn the ancient thatch
Upon the lonely moated grange.

And what a living portrait the keen observation gives us here:

Ther was also a Nonne, a Prioresse,
That of hir smyling was ful simple and coy;
Hir gretteste ooth was but by Sëynt Loy;
And she was cleped Madame Eglentyne.
Ful wel she sang the service devyne,
Entuned in hir nose ful semely;
And Frensh she spak ful faire and fetisly,
After the scole of Stratford atte Bowe,
For Frensh of Paris was to hir unknowe.
At mete well y-taught was she with-alle;
She leet no morsel from hir lippes falle,
Ne wette hir fingres in hir sauce depe.
Wel coude she carie a morsel, and wel kepe,
That no drope ne fille upon her brest.

There again we see how close humour is to poetry in its vision and keenness of observation.

To take one more example, in the *Eve of St. Agnes* a few words can make us hear "the elfin

storm from fairyland'' and feel ourselves escaping
with the lovers:

> Down the wide stairs a darkling way they found.
> In all the house was heard no human sound.
> A chain-drooped lamp was flickering by each door;
> The arras, rich with horseman, hawk and hound,
> Flutter'd in the besieging wind's uproar;
> And the long carpets rose along the gusty floor.

If we recall the descriptive pictures which remain clearest in our minds we shall find that those
we have been given by the poets are not only the
most beautiful and unforgettable but also the
most accurate in observation.

We have noted that a good deal of ostensible
poetry is really prose. To speak only of great
names we find this in most of the work of Horace,
of Racine and Corneille, of Dryden and Pope, in
much of *The Excursion* and in the longer poems
of Browning. A word may be said about the
passages in prose form which are really poetry.
Two things will be discovered in examining these,
—firstly, that the conception is emotional and
imaginative, and secondly, that the language is
rhythmical and is indeed a subtle form of verse.
I give two examples from the hundreds that might

be cited. This is from Sir Ector's lament for Sir Lancelot:

"Ah Lancelot", he said, "thou were the head of all Christian Knights. And thou were the courtliest Knight that ever bear shield. And thou were the truest friend to thy lover that ever bestrode horse. And thou were the truest lover of a sinful man that ever loved woman. And thou were the kindest man that ever struck with sword. And thou were the goodliest person that ever came among press of Knights. And thou were the meekest man and the gentlest that ever ate in hall among ladies. And thou were the sternest Knight to thy mortal foe that ever put spear in rest.

And this from the Book of Common Prayer:

O God we have heard with our ears, and our fathers have declared unto us, the noble works that thou didst in their days, and in the old time before them.

Science is the reading of life through investigation: poetry the reading of life through the imagination. Religion is the reading of life through belief in a divine revelation; philosophy its reading through an impartial and balanced consideration of all other interpretations.

While scientific theories, religious creeds, and philosophic systems change, the essential quality of poetry remains the same: it is a vision of the

eternal wonder and beauty that dwells at the
heart of life. The vision persists: scientific knowledge may alter man's point of view, but poetry
accepts and absorbs the discoveries of science and
gives wings to its facts. We may have to pay with
our dreams for the truth we win from knowledge,
but the knowledge we win opens new pathways
into wonderland and leads us again to a dream.
The imagination gives to naked reality what the
atmosphere gives to the terrestrial scene. It may
sometimes disguise but it seldom fails to reveal,
and the dreams of poetry become the interpreters
of truth:

> Dreams that give to the thing life shows
> What the Sky gives Earth, when the evening glows
>   On the distant hills, and the lonely places
> Blossom in gold and purple and rose.

"We are such stuff as dreams are made on", but
poetry has interpreted those dreams as memories
or premonitions of eternal truth,—not as night-
mares. The great poets, the Seers, have always
taken a brave and trustful view of life; they have
never eyed "a beauteous face in a cracked glass".
Only in the sight of the smaller and self-centred
has the conception of life been ignoble.

241

No mean interpretation of life, no mere utilitarian explanation of human ideals, has found
permanent expression in poetry. The great and
beautiful creations of man in Art are expressions
of a noble conception; and it is inspiriting to
believe that these great conceptions are not the
mere outcome of his wishes, not his dreams of
something finer than what is, but the revelation
of a reality which exists beyond the evident,—an
illumination, not a veiling of truth.

IX

OUR ISLAND WORLD

IX

OUR ISLAND WORLD

AMONG the countless worlds in the visible universe we have been shown nothing that suggests intercourse or community, no bond between those possible homes of life comparable to contact between nation and nation, or even between scattered outposts in lonely lands. Each world seems to be isolated and divided by impassable gulfs of space from the others.

In a world so large that its boundaries had never been found by its inhabitants the isolation would be little felt. Beyond its known limits there would always be new fields for discovery, new clues to the mystery of creation. On us, dwellers on the Earth, the isolation is forcibly impressed by the smallness of our world. We know it: no land remains untraversed, no sea uncharted, and beyond it we have nowhere to go.

In modern times this has been still farther emphasised by the facilities and speed of transport. Steamships and trains and aeroplanes, cables and wireless telegraphy have brought the remotest parts of the earth into intimacy, and scenes in lands whose inaccessibility once endowed them with mystery are now familiar through the cinema, to people who are imprisoned in crowded towns. It is a sort of familiarity which is in danger of breeding contempt, a conveyance of knowledge, a presentation of reality which arrives at second hand and has lost the animation of personal contact.

To-day we have to face the fact that man's limited habitation is shrinking under the magic of his mechanical progress, and the permanent wonder of life itself is being obscured to his vision by the dazzling light of his own inventions. Though this adventurous progress may deserve approval, we deserve nothing but contempt for our lack of judgment in guiding it, and for the ruthlessness and greed with which we have mutilated our fair dwelling-place in our utilitarian activities.

"Forget six counties overhung with smoke", said William Morris fifty years ago. To-day there is much more that he would bid us forget. But let us free our imagination from the oppression of these miscarriages of progress: let us rather remember the abiding magnificence of our home on

246

earth and read life in the light of its scenes of perennial wonder and beauty. Let us make a voyage of discovery, not like our ancestors in search of new lands, but to look, as though for the first time, on the seas and shores whose names are familiar to us.

First I would take you with me to a time when we were younger and the world was wider than it is to-day. And the voyage is on a sailing-ship, which, if it does not provide the luxuries of a hotel and wireless reports from the Stock Exchanges, will carry us through enchanted seas that are never seen from the decks of a liner. From the hour when we cast off our tug in the English Channel and are away under our own sail, we are separated from the modern world and all its temporal interests. Almost at once we begin to look at the world with new eyes. That land we see over the grey waters, its fields sloping to the shore, its havens between the headlands, is England, but not the England of the newspapers and the motor roads. A few hours, a few miles of separation have restored to it some immemorial quality and given perspective to our imaginations. We forget the popular watering-places as we pass the coast marks whose names have been in the

247

ears of sailors for centuries—the North Foreland and Dungeness, Beachy Head and Selsey Bill, and the thronged waterways of Spithead. We may try to look on the scene as though for the first time: those grey-green waves are running to the shore exactly as they did in eighteenth-century seas, but we cannot forget their story: their beauty is unchanged but the story of the three-deckers that once anchored on their waters is written into that beauty. The world we are going to see is smaller than that which our ancestors explored, but every part of it now contains a story which may give to its scenes an expansion in time which may be some compensation for what is lost in space.

No other path can take the traveller so far from the surroundings of modern life or bring him so closely into contact with the untamed forces of Nature as that of a sailing-ship. His course is far from the frequented modern highways of navigation, and for weeks no vessel may be sighted. Our ship is dependent on wind and weather and has to encounter dangers from which the large steamer is generally secure. A liner is driven on an unchanged course through head seas in gales of wind, and there is something like an angry contention between her and the elements as she cleaves her onward way with green seas breaking over her bows and her propellers racing in the air. A sailing-ship is a thing born of the elements, not of the fitting-shop; she has taken shape and found equipment to make alliance with the winds and adapt her movements to those of the waters. In the fury of a hurricane you might be glad to exchange her wave-swept decks for the drawing-room of a liner, but to know the sea and man's contact with its realities you must have experienced the triumph of a storm outsailed on a sailing-ship, and feel the delight of her movements in responding to the embraces of a fair wind and running seas.

Our voyage to the Antipodes round the Cape of Good Hope takes us first on a south-westerly course, and the last of the home shores to be seen is Cape Clear. Finisterre, being on the Continent, may really be the land's-end of Europe, but Ireland throws a farewell promontory still further into the Atlantic. Our ship carried about twenty steerage emigrants and among them was a middle-aged Irishman, a widower who with two boys and a girl was leaving his barren holding to join his eldest son in Australia in the hope of giving

his children a better chance in life. As a fellow
countryman I had made friends with them and I
happened to be standing beside the father as we
had our last look at Ireland. To me, who expected
in due course to return, that farewell awakened
some emotion, but to him, who knew that there
was little hope of his ever seeing Ireland again,
the pain was almost unbearable. I remembered
that he was but one of tens of thousands who
take that last look at their native land, and I
wondered whether, after all, there may not be
compensation for the narrowed dimensions of our
island world in the homeliness of its limitations,
and the shortening of every homeward path for
the exile. There is something almost tragic in the
transplanting of people to foreign scenes,—almost
literally a tearing-up of roots when they are taken
from a place where their ancestors have lived, a
place from whose characteristics their own have
been formed. From the English village, from the
lough side in Connemara, from the Swiss mountains, to the factory or hotel in Chicago or New
York is almost like a transition to another world
and would be unbearable if it were not for the
sympathy and comradeship which exists everywhere between human beings and awaits the new-

comer in strange lands. If we were told that instead of death an interminable exile to some remote and alien land, beyond the forests of Siberia or the mountains of Thibet awaited us,— should we not choose death in preference? It is human love and sympathy that gives the emigrant hope and courage,—and it is only such faith as we may have in the permanence of the ties we have formed on earth that makes the prospect of survival after death attractive. A dying man's backward look on the life he is leaving is something like that of the emigrant on the only home he knows.

One week of sailing has already enlarged the spaces of our world and impressed us with the immensity of the ocean. We begin to realise the fact that three-fifths of the earth's surface is sea and that beneath our little ship are depths equal to the height of the highest mountains. Room enough in those oceans for more continents but how much better it is that they are unfilled,—for they remain a permanent refuge from the congestion and spoilation of the multitude; and their vast reservoirs preserve the whole earth from the dangers of pollution. Drawn to the skies their waters are distilled and fall in rain on the land,

to flow back in rivers to their fountain source;
and even when the river waters have been fouled
by drains and factories to be made sweet again in
their renewal. But how differently we look at the
world. I once asked an American lady who had
just crossed the Atlantic if she liked the sea. "The
Ocean!" she replied, "I despise it."

The exquisite green of shallow seas has passed
into the dark blue of deep ocean. No sail, no land
has met our outlook. Obedient to the ruling of
the winds our course has been more southerly than
usual, and on the tenth morning of our voyage the
blue outline of mountains breaks the ring of horizon waters, and in the evening we are sailing close
to island shores. No exaggeration of old mariners,
no imagined picture of islands, "fabled within the
Atlantic main", could overvalue the loveliness of
that vision. Mountains, wooded half-way to their
summits, broken by deep ravines, rise from mid-
ocean, and the long ocean swell lifts and falls along
their rocky plinths. You can hardly tell where the
masonry of Nature ends and man's begins, for the
little port we are nearing seems like a buttress of
the mountains with its foundation in the sea. And
the whole scene is glorified by a magnificence of
colour such as few of us have ever seen before.

The sea has won it from the sky and the land is transfigured between them. The deep dark ocean blue is crossed by violet shadows and passes into pale green under the rock ledges; against the dark green of the mountain slopes the evening sun lights the golden terraces of the climbing town and the crimson tapestry of flowers that hang from the garden walls. Then as the twilight falls and the colours slowly darken and are lost on the lower levels the distant heights still hail the western glow and a rosy mist enfolds their summits.

What dreamland is this? The Isles of the Hesperides? Tir n'an oge? We could picture Ulysses or the Argonauts sailing into that haven. And the answer seems an anti-climax. This is Madeira, and on a South African liner you may reach it in comfort in five days. That fairy palace whose lights we see shining through the trees is Reid's Hotel, and if we had come here in a more sensible way we should probably be over-dining there and afterwards find our way down to the Casino. But our enchanted voyage would have come to an end.

And now our course is south-westward across the ocean plains, fields of the old sea wars and routes of galleons laden with silver store from the

Spanish Main, but to-day an unfrequented solitude
of lonely waters.

At Flores in the Azores Sir Richard Grenville lay—

and somewhere here

*The little Revenge herself went down by the island crags
To be lost evermore in the main.*

Over the blue horizon rings we pass our days of
monotonous and lovely sequence and nights of un-
paralleled magnificence. From this outpost in the
ocean we look into the depths of half the universe;
and never in our northern latitudes have the stars
shone so luminously and at the same time so
clearly shown their sphericity; never did the distances that separate them from each other and
from us seem so profound. The sea around us is
dark, the decks of the ship are dark: against the
starlight the topmasts gently rise and fall: we
seem to be outside or beyond the world we knew,
sailing through immensities of space. We are on
a voyage to see our island home, but the view out-
wards, the view of the heavens which it allows us
from its windows, is the most amazing part of the
scenery. If, like the planet Venus, the earth had
been enfolded in a cloud canopy, or attended by

satellites that gave constant illumination to the night, man would never have known that there were any spheres of life beyond the earth. That outlook, though it may make us feel the smallness of our island of life, nevertheless exalts us in our apprehension of the stupendous creation of which we are part. Looking out from the dark decks of our ship, from the dark ocean floor of our world into those immense realms of life, we are lost in amazement, amazement at the miracle of sight which allows us to see the spheres which are separated from us by almost unimaginable distances, at that even greater vision of the mind which has given us knowledge of the laws that guide the courses of those spheres: at the courage of the spirit which can set out hopefully into the unknown in quest of truth.

Our own astronomical observations may, of course, be confined to remote regions of creation, and it may be possible that nearer its fountain springs there may be systems in which communication exists between world and world. As to this science has not been able to enlighten us. In the case of the Solar system its physical conditions suggest that life on the other planets is improbable though not impossible. Looking beyond it

255

we have no evidence that a single one of those
innumerable worlds is inhabited, but to conclude
that none of them is inhabited would be preposterous,—indeed it is reasonable to suppose that
there are worlds superior not only in size but in
excellence to our Earth, worlds in which the
beauty and significance of the scenery of life are
beyond our powers of imagination. If we try to
picture these I think we shall come nearest to the
truth if we assume that their essential conditions
are not unlike those which we have found on our
own sphere, that they are governed by physical
laws which are universal, that, where mind has
been born, reason is invariable, that what we call
the essential values, truth and goodness and
beauty, are the same as revealed to us, that the
stage may be exalted but the themes of the play
inspired by kindred passions of the heart and
adventures of the spirit; that though there may
be no physical communication between the
worlds, there is a community in the conscious
life of the universe.

All this is speculation, albeit reasoned speculation, but we may accept, as far as exploration of
the universe has been possible, the conclusion that
its worlds, its homes of life are isolated, and that

each of them must read its destiny within the limits of its own boundaries.

The wonder, the possibilities, the immeasurable significance of the life we find on Earth justify our imaginative flights in picturing worlds of greater activities. Life itself is the miracle: given this we need not be timid about its extension. We can imagine that one of those points of light marks a world which is so large that its confines have never been discovered by its inhabitants; and if we picture ourselves looking out into the heavens from that world we should see very much the same scene as is revealed to us here: the same immeasurable depths, the same stars though arranged in a somewhat different pattern, and perhaps some new vista into what seems to be the illimitable regions of creation. To the inhabitants of that nobler sphere these visions would have the same mystery as they have for us. However great the scope for expansion within their boundaries, the secret of life would lie beyond them, and like us, they would be driven to seek the solution within their own spirits. I am suggesting that the life of intelligent beings in other worlds would not be fundamentally different from our own, that we are not to picture worlds inhabited by creatures like super-insects, with qualities hostile to our ideals, that no conscious being would find himself a spiritual alien if transferred to another of the habitable spheres, and that the whole universe is one great Commonwealth of life—

> This truth within thy mind rehearse
> That in a boundless universe
> Is boundless better, boundless worse.

No! It ought to have been said not "this truth", but "this untruth". The good is creative, the evil self-destructive. We cannot measure the expansion of the good, but we can see that evil with its accompaniments of pain and futility has limits and invariably leads to dissolution. We have pictured spheres where the evolution of life has been nobler and more beautiful, has extended farther than on this earth: we may picture other spheres which are in a cruder state of development, but we can picture none on which the meaner, the crueller, the fouler aspects of life have risen to triumphant achievement. We have learned on Earth that the wages of sin is death.

What a contrast between the inconceivable magnitude of the heavens into which we have been looking and the narrow space of our little ship, our only present foothold in the universe,—

a frail thing on whose sea-worthiness we depend for our existence! From those far-reaching speculations we come back to our little community of fellow travellers with a sense of comfort: their presence gives a homeliness to the vast. We feel that we are united to the life beyond our knowledge as much by personal sympathy as by physical laws, that courage and love and beauty and humour are as elemental as gravitation, that on the farthest sphere the stout-heartedness of our seamen would awaken admiration, the ribald jests of the forecastle provoke laughter, our Irish emigrant's love of country touch a chord of sympathy, and that the lovely message of life, won from the mountains and rivers of Kerry, that shone in the eyes of his little daughter would need no interpretation in distant worlds, being written in the beauty which is the one universal language.

We are on our way to the Cape of Good Hope, but have sailed on an erratic course via the starry depths of the universe. We have passed the sea plains over which the heavens shone so gloriously, we have run before the north-east trade wind till we were almost in sight of the South American continent. We have been becalmed in the Sargasso Sea among the floating patches of sea-weed

inhabited by minute crabs, wandering islands in
the ocean, but hardly more lonely and remote than
our own island Earth in the depths of space.

Hitherto we have experienced only the delights
of a voyage in a sailing-ship. We have seen the
friendly aspects of the great ocean, but now we
were to learn the stupendous fury of its antagonism. Down in the "Roaring Forties", goaded by
a constant succession of gales, the seas hurl themselves eastward round the Earth. To-day, the
voyage to Chili and Peru and California is through
the Panama Canal, a pleasant water excursion: the
sight of the southern ocean makes us marvel at the
courage and endurance of the old navigators who
had to beat their way to those lands round the
Horn. On our own course for the Cape of Good
Hope we had the advantage of those westerly
gales while they remained moderate, and the
change from summer seas to wilder waters was
exhilarating. At first the skies were cloudless and
the great following seas were a deep blue, green-
crested where the sunlight shot through them.
Then, when the force of the wind increased, came
the order to shorten sail and everyone on board
entered into the spirit of the coming encounter.
I have never beheld a more thrilling scene than

that of the little ship riding those great seas,
and the men aloft reefing topsails, their bodies
stretched over the yards, with no other security
than the support of the foot-ropes, nor shall I
ever hear braver music than that of their chanties,
sung while they were swinging on the halyards
from the deck:

> The times are bad and the wages low,
> Leave her, Johnny, leave her!
> We scrubbed the decks in the watch below,
> And its time for us to leave her.
>
> She had a dark and a rolling eye,
> Leave her, Johnny, leave her!

—and so on for as long as was needed, the first
line ringing out in solo, then all together with the
burden as they swung on the ropes, and all mingled
with the tumult of the wind and the waves.

The full force of the gale came two days later
when we were somewhere south of the Cape. The
seas had begun to break dangerously over the ship's
quarter and for general safety we were hauled up
as near the wind as was possible, carrying no
canvas but, I believe, a couple of staysails. I have
never been in a serious earthquake, and can
imagine that this must be Earth's most terrifying

spectacle, but I believe that nothing can equal in its appalling grandeur the upheaval of the ocean and the onrush of its stupendous waves, that nowhere but in a ship, alone in those seas, can man find himself so isolated and shelterless in the midst of the elemental forces.

Under a barrage of driving rain the huge billows were almost hidden until they were towering above us. Time after time it looked as if they must crash down on the decks, and time after time the beautiful ship rose to their lift, and away they went, swirling along her sides and hissing under her stern. Now and again a green sea broke over her bows and the decks were awash. There were two men at the wheel and the captain hardly left his station on the poop for two days; but however great our danger may have been, he did not seem in the least perturbed. "She's taking it quite comfortable", was his comment, but he afterwards told us a different story. Through those days we watched with a fearful fascination the assault of the massed forces of the oncoming seas, but it was as night fell and we saw them no more but only heard the sound of the wind wailing through the shrouds, and the rush of the seas all round us, that we felt the full awe of our isolation in that lonely waste of waters. It is an experience no one may wish for twice, but having come through it once and seen the bravery and resource of the men who cheerfully face its dangers, from the master of the ship to the roughest blackguard in his crew, we can feel a human pride in realising that man has stuff in his heart which is worthy to be matched with the grandest forces that Nature can bring against him.

We lost our fore-topmast in that encounter and one poor fellow was washed overboard. The damage necessitated going into port for repairs, and as soon as the weather permitted we made our course for Durban and crossed the bar of that pleasant haven a few days later.

> What if some little pain the passage have
> That makes frail flesh to feare the bitter wave,
> Is not short paine well borne that brings long ease?

You must have been through the stress of the elemental contest, and heard the wild battle-calls of winds and waters, to know the blessed peace of a sheltered haven. Outside the bar we could still hear the distant boom of the breakers, but around us the only sounds that touched the silence came from the dip of an oar, a ship's bell, or the ripple of the tide under our bows. The smell of the earth, of unfamiliar vegetation and flowers, was borne on the night air; never had the lights of houses looked so homely as those which shone along the harbour, never stars so tranquil as those we saw reflected in the still waters of our anchorage.

And this was Africa! the dark enchanted continent of antiquity, that still holds a spirit of mystery and wonder more potent than any unexplored region of the new world. Still? At least it was so for us who reached its shores on that voyage of rediscovery so many years ago. That little port, half hidden in sub-tropical vegetation, its two thoroughfares sandy tracks between the outer ocean and the bush-covered hills, its cross streets just garden-paths running down to the edge of the lagoon; with its primitive stores, its wagons drawn by teams of bullocks, its mixed population, British, Dutch, natives from Zululand and coolies from India, the bush land, which sheltered wild animals, growing in primeval wildness within a few miles of the town,—in none of it was there anything to disturb the romance of all that is held in the word *Africa*. But that was long ago. Now Durban is a fine city; in the old garden streets

there are large hotels and cinemas; now the lovely
highlands of Natal are scarred with the battle-
fields of an unjust war where brave British and
Boer soldiers lie side by side in their graves; now
through those lands of mystery the railway runs to
the gold-mines and the cosmopolitan vulgarity of
Johannesburg.

Much of the old mystery and romance has gone,
but much remains. On that voyage of rediscovery, blown from our intended course we find
ourselves in one of the oldest homes of man and
the nobler wild animals,—dwellers side by side
in something like neighbourliness. New wonders
greet us everywhere, and in our admiration we
are disturbed by the reflection that modern progress should decree the destruction of so much
that Nature has taken so long and shown such
surpassing skill in shaping. Looked at from the
point of view of a visitor from another sphere,
how much more fascinating a world would be
beheld in those native haunts of the wild creatures
and the primitive activities of man than in the
crowded cities and manufacturing areas of civilisation. Here he would see in the lion and antelope
an expression of life which has its own perfected
nobility and beauty. Man is capable of spiritual

and moral progress, and remains a very imperfect being, but in the lion and the deer Nature has completed a magnificent bit of artistic work. Our visitor would also see a humorous record of Nature's activities in the monkey, the alligator, and the hippopotamus, and an embodiment of her loveliest dreams in the plumage of the birds that flash between the flowering trees of the bush. Here, too, he would see a race of men who had something of the nobility of their surroundings, —the Zulu, a creature of magnificent physique, brave and upright in conduct, without craft or subtlety of intellect, happy among native races in that he has not yet been corrupted by a civilisation whose triumphs would be lost on him, but whose vices are contagious. In this contemplation the narrow limits of our world are again brought home to us: we are filled with regret that it is not large enough to provide new fields for its multiplying peoples without destroying the irreplaceable wonder and beauty of its primeval sanctuaries.

The scene of this primitive life is superb. Blue distances, wider than ocean's, fill the eye. Wild pageantries of storm cross the heavens. After an azure morning a cloud no bigger than a man's hand appears on the horizon of the hills and spreads with amazing rapidity until the whole sky is obscured. Like drums of an advancing host comes the roll of thunder, the storm-clouds are piled like black citadels, and the lightning plays round their turrets in golden chains, and flashes earthward in javelin strokes. Then Earth and skies are commingled; in a crash of thunder the pinnacles of cloud fall inward and the sound of rushing rain hushes the reverberating peal. In an hour or two the rivers have filled and go roaring in flood to meet the breakers of the Indian Ocean, and in a couple of hours it is all over. An exquisite calm follows, and while you can still hear the thunder far away northward as the storm passes over the Tugela Valley or round the heights of the Drakensberg the sunset is lighting the western skies with hues of crimson and gold.

It is a larger, grander scene of life than any we know in our northern latitudes. Our elemental disturbances come to us in long dark days of rain that falls dismally on the streets of towns, or snows that drift across forlorn moors,—and yet, from those days are born others of incomparable loveliness and joy,—winter days of crystal frost and filtered air that brace the heart; days of spring and summer when the breeze is sweet with the smell of the earth and the grass and the wild flowers, days that hold a spirit that seems nearer the beauty at the heart of life than any that dawn elsewhere.

To feel this is good. Every man's native country is nearer than any other to the fountain-springs of life. We have memories that possess our hearts, but our vision of those South African lands has shown us new glories of our island world and added something to our terrestrial pride.

Our course from Durban to Australia was northward of the stormy latitudes, and with fair westerly winds and one moderate gale we crossed that vast southern ocean in which is no land except the island of Kerguelen, which we left far to the south, and where we had no fellow travellers but the great albatrosses that swept along beside us like embodied crests of the waves. We saw the first land, the south-east coast of Tasmania, four weeks after our departure from Durban, and a week later we passed through the Heads into Sydney Harbour.

The latest-discovered continents are the least interesting, and there are few parts of the Earth that have so little beauty and romance as Aus-

tralia. The skies above it, the blue Pacific waters
that enter its harbours are superb, but the land
itself is tame. The heart of the continent is desert,
the coastal regions monotonous tracts of gum
forest. You feel here that modern exploitation is
not an intrusion but an improvement, and that
the enterprise and hard work of the colonists who
have felled the woods and brought the land into
cultivation, who have introduced new varieties of
vegetation, who have mined the gold and iron and
made prosperous homes for their kin, have built
up much that is permanently good and destroyed
little that was worth keeping.

There is not an interesting wild animal in the
country, not a bird in the woods that has a song,
not a fish in the rivers that will take a fly; and the
aboriginal natives, who are gradually dying off, are
contemptible creatures that needed extermination.
It is a country which man must make, and is making. These Australians of British stock have taken
in hand a piece of work that needed human energy
to give this part of the earth real value, and they
have re-created it. There are no ancient monu-
ments to deface, no lovely scenes to mar: man
here may have his progressive fling without
hesitation; cities may expand without destruc-

tiveness, motor roads may intersect the country and pylons punctuate the landscape without offence: all the beauty which is possible to modernity may be developed.

Sydney Harbour, the finest anchorage in the world, is not beautiful apart from the charm of its deep-blue waters. Gum trees and villas are interspersed along its low coast-line and no salient feature on the shore attracts the eye. But at night it is a fairy scene of modern artificial making. Those tranquil waters hold reflected in their depths the lights of a magic city, and are crossed in every direction by the scintillating flash of enchanted ferry-boats. Our visitor from another sphere looking on that scene might indeed think he had found one of Earth's loveliest and most romantic places,—and even when he learned that the effect was due to electric light and that the people in the ferry-boats were satisfied in listening to vulgar music on gramophones, the beauty of the scene would still remain, indeed might seem to be prophetic of the still more brilliant spectacles which man may create in the future, when the galleons of the air float across these waters, and drop fairy music from Aeolian dulcimers.

Advance Australia! advance in man's latest progressive ventures; and in doing so, having no natural glories to preserve, may you be thoughtful in your constructive energies. Pause ere you try to emulate the forbidding altitudes of American building; and, having room to spare, make your cities and garden suburbs, your factories and playgrounds, splendid in themselves.

And now our voyage in the old sailing-ship is over and we have to say good-bye to our fellow travellers with whom our narrow boundaries have brought us into such close comradeship. There were tears in the eyes of my emigrant countryman when we parted: he knew I should see the old places again and clung to me as a link with them. He will not return and his little daughter will marry and transmit some of the beauty of the mountains and streams, that had passed into her face, to children of her new homeland.

Having travelled as far as it is possible from our native land, who could have foreseen that instead of finding ourselves in totally foreign surroundings we should reach shores which were more like our own than any others on Earth? You might easily think that Wellington Harbour was a Scottish sea loch, and after landing you would meet men and women of the best classes, gentle and simple, that the old country has bred, and hear speech uncorrupted by Cockney decadence or American stridency.

How wonderful a thing is the bond of race: New Zealand, farther from the British shores than any country in the world, is nearer to them than France. Out on the hills of one of the stations where the grass-lands are broken by patches of furze and broom you will hear voices that carry you back to the Highlands of Scotland; the sons of your host, who are working side by side with the shepherds and shearers, have been home to a university; the magnificent rough life of the day is followed by evenings which maintain the refinements of an old aristocracy.

There are patrician peasantries, just as there are plebeian ascendencies: you find the former in Ireland and the Highlands of Scotland, in the Tyrol and many another old country. In New Zealand the best traditions of class are fused in a new freedom and relationship. New Zealand is one of the most democratic countries in the world and yet one of the best-governed. Democracy can only be successful when the people are really aristocratic. If we are to have good government directed by a majority, that majority must be composed of the best elements in the community.

This country of beautiful highlands, pleasant pastures, and clear running rivers,—of scattered homesteads and small towns, allowing community without congestion,—New Zealand makes us realise how much more fortunate is man when he and Nature are in friendly relationship than when he has blackened the earth's surface with factories, disembowelled it in mines and imprisoned himself in the streets of dreary towns.

The happy pastoral shores of New Zealand have been the text for these reflections. They make us feel how fine a thing it would be for man if there were lands like these still awaiting discovery,—continents where there would be room for the growing populations of the world. Possession is good for man as long as it is not acquired by the dispossession of others. It is not in the corporate life, not as one of an urban population who lives in a street and is a shareholder in museums and public parks and gardens, that a man becomes a person, but in places where he owns a part of the Earth, however small, places which he loves and on which he stamps his character.

And now I would take you with me into very different scenes. A week's journey from Auckland

on a little vessel trading in copra, brings us among
the South Sea Islands and shows us some of the
dreams of our boyhood. Coral islands, treasure
islands, pirates, friendly natives, how near all this
wonderland seemed to us in the stories we read,—
how much nearer, and how much more wonderful
than now when we are in it! And here,—if I may
again interpose a reflection,—I would say how
good it is that our realisations never come up to
our expectations. If they did we should stagnate
in content; but imagination sends us forth un-
satisfied on voyages of eternal discovery.

Though the South Sea Islands may not fulfil
our youthful dreams of their enchantment, they
have a pleasing and indolent loveliness. Most of
them hardly rise above sea-level, and the palm
trees that you sight on the horizon as you approach
seem to spring from the ocean itself. In some of
them, such as Samoa, there is a mountain glory,
but most of them owe their charm to their ocean
setting, and nowhere in the world is there such
beauty of water as in the coral basins inside the
island reefs.

There is a cave in a cliff in Vavau, large as the
dome of a cathedral, where the glory and variety
of blue flash in changing light through still waters

a hundred feet deep, yet so clear that you can see the pebbles on the coral floor; and on the dome above, covered with pink moss, blue lights are thrown from the depths and make patterns on the roof like rays from a stained-glass window.

At home we know the sea as a fringe of the land: here in the Pacific the land is just an incident in the sea.

The island natives have a fine physique, fine manners, and some decorative taste. In our northern races among unlovely scenes we constantly see faces of men and women in which there is revelation of a beauty far transcending their surroundings; but here Nature seems to have found consummation of expression in a creature, a happy animal which is conscious of its pleasant if mortal conditions and desires no other; and the content and limitations are written in his countenance.

Wandering among the islands, sitting with chiefs under the ovava trees, drinking khava, fanned by maidens clad in hibiscus blossoms, bathing in the coral pools, we might expect soon to forget all our traditions and immortal hopes, and recognise in this happy consciousness of life, this easy gratification of the senses, and gentle declination to death, the fulfilment of man's

destiny. But, No! That dream would be short-
lived. In sterner surroundings, in conflict and
danger, the stronger race of mankind to which we
belong have proved themselves the creators, not
the creatures of their circumstances, and for them
no bounded earthly paradise could bring content.

Nowhere has the romance of travel been so truly
expressed as in the writings of Robert Louis
Stevenson. He set out in search of his dreams,
and though he did not find them in any destination they always led him on. Indeed he said, "It
is better to travel hopefully than to arrive". Long
ago, when I was a young man, I had the privilege
of being his guest at Vailima in Samoa. I had been
drifting among the islands, receiving idle impressions and wondering as I approached Samoa
whether a man who had lived for any length of
time in "a land in which it seemed always after-
noon" could escape its influence or produce
vigorous work. But from the road that led upward
through the tropical forest I passed through the
gates of Vailima into the north country; and in an
hour after finding myself in Stevenson's company
I was in a world of movement and activity, of
brave effort and stimulating ideas. The silence of
the forest enfolded us, the great blue ring of un-

troubled ocean lay below, and the hush of waters on the reef reached our ears; but now the atmosphere seemed to belong to bracing north-eastern coasts, and windy mornings on the moors.

As our world grows smaller we may be thankful to those who make our life in it larger; to those who, like Stevenson, give us new horizons of the spirit and discover for us treasure islands in the human heart.

So that mountain-slope in Samoa where Stevenson ended his earthly travels remains the most memorable scene to me in the islands. No man lived more generously than he, and none could ask for a happier requiem:

> Under the wide and starry sky
> Dig the grave and let me lie.
> Glad did I live and gladly die,
>   And I laid me down with a will.
>
> This be the verse you grave for me:
> Here he lies where he longed to be;
> Home is the sailor, home from sea,
>   And the hunter home from the hill.

On a fascinating voyage inside the great Australian Barrier Reef, over the waters of the pearl fishers, onward through the Spice Islands, with a call at Manila, where we are reminded how far the old Spanish adventurers reached by seeing monastic buildings of the sixteenth century, we sail northward out of lovely comatose regions into a new world of human activity.

If you had romantic conceptions of Japan they will soon be dissipated, for its people are the most prosaic and materialistic in the world. The country itself has beautiful natural features, but almost everything that man can do to mar its beauty has been done by its over-population. We have heard of it as the land of the lotus and chrysanthemum, a garden of blossoming trees. We find a country in which there are no grass-lands, no wild flowers, where there are no animals except cows and draft oxen, where the birds have been exterminated. It is true that the cherry and other fruit trees have been intensively cultivated for their bloom, and some of the old villages nestling in clouds of white and pink blossom are amazingly picturesque; but the thatched roofs are being everywhere replaced by iron, and when the spring flowering season is over there is little to admire. Much of the land is barren and the forests of cryptomaria, without wild animal or bird, are depressing. In remote districts we come upon old-world unspoilt places,

278

mountain solitudes, with villages with thatched
houses beside a stream that turns a water-mill,
mysterious temples in dark groves,—but in the
fertile valley-lands where the huge population is
concentrated, the least pleasing forms of modern
innovation have banished natural charm and
erased the graciousness of old-world architecture.
Here between town and town there is no interval
of country; the towns are connected by roads lined
on either side by houses at the back of which are
land allotments, used for the intensive cultivation
of vegetables. And the whole country smells like
an open drain. The Japanese have been forced by
circumstances to practise extreme economy, and
like the termites, make use of their own excre-
ment, which is carried out in buckets every morning and deposited on the garden plot.

The Japanese are a people with whom it is
almost impossible for Europeans to enter into
comradeship. They have qualities of mind which
enable them to adopt fully the world's mechanical
advance; they are quick in adaptation and capable
of self-denial in their aims, which are almost
wholly utilitarian. When they decided to modern-
ise their country they did so deliberately. It is
said they sent commissions through the world to

ascertain which countries should be their exem-
plars in the reorganisation of their national life,
and as a consequence adopted the naval system of
Great Britain, the military system of Germany,
and the educational system of the United States.
On religion the commission reported that there
was no country whose religion had borne any fruit
in the conduct of the people that was of account,
and that there was nothing to be gained by changing their own. A cold logical utilitarianism regu-
lates their daily life. Reason untouched by sentiment or moral ideals decides their habits from the
training of children to the supervision of national
brothels, where the women are exhibited like
manikins in the shop-fronts of selected streets
and graded and priced like merchandise. They
possess in a high degree those qualities of mind
which find fulfilment in mechanical progress, but
they are deficient in those qualities of the spirit
which ennoble life. You feel that you are among
creatures which have been evolved from the insect
rather than from the animal, and that there is
much in their community that corresponds with
that of the ants. If the spiritual forces in the
world become smothered by the utilitarian, and
mechanical progress is unrestrained, the Japanese

will be among the fittest to survive.

In the evolution of the insect, Nature seems to have found a cul-de-sac. In the ant and the bee we see the complete suppression of the individual in the interest of the community,—but this restriction of freedom has resulted in a finality of accomplishment beyond which there is no progress. In the national life of other countries than Japan which are subordinating individual liberty to the dictatorship of a government we may see a kinship with these insect communities and can discover in their organisations no egress for the progressive spirit of man.

In our voyage over the earth we have realised as we never could before how small a world it is, and also what an amazing amount it contains. The track we have come by was a long and leisurely one: returning by a more direct route, the dimensions of the earth seem still smaller. A fortnight in a liner across the Pacific, a week in a train across America, another week on the Atlantic and we should be at home again; or if we returned westward on the comfortable decks of a P. & O. steamer we should need but a week longer.

To travel back through America would be to embark on a new voyage of discovery, but though we turn away we cannot escape from the magnetic influence of the concentration of human energy that flows from that source into every part of the world. It is an energy which has not yet been nobly directed, and has been so far chiefly utilitarian; but in the National Being of the United States there is a heart of idealism which, if it can achieve expression, will redeem and re-create the whole structure of the New World. Hitherto America has been so absorbed in the development of its own great territories, and the nationalisation of its peoples, that unlike the countries which have had to seek fields for emigration, she has hardly looked beyond the horizons of her own shores; but now she, too, is beginning to realise the limitations of the space on Earth and recognise that the problems of the world are hers also. Her cosmopolitan nationality, which hitherto has been a weakness, may become an ultimate strength, and it may enable her to take a specially sympathetic and prominent part in bringing the nations of the world together.

In the life of this new world of America pathways are opening whose goals we cannot foresee.

We must leave them now unentered, and pursue
our homeward journey, touching the shores of old
countries whose names are so familiar to us and
whose people we know so little. China and India,
Arabia and Egypt, and the immemorial sea-ways
of the Mediterranean. Of these lands we shall have
but glimpses, and we shall learn before the end of
our journey that those who would see the earth
by sailing round it in a liner would gain little
more knowledge of it than if they had been looking at cinema pictures on a pier in a British water-
ing-place. And in a few years the survey will be
made easier still by the help of television: without
moving, our spectators will be able to exclaim with
Little Billee, when he climbed to the main-top-
gallant mast,

> There's Jerusalem and Madagascar
> And North and South Amerikee.

Our first port of call is Hong Kong. On the
confines of Asia, set on the mysterious border of
the Orient, it is humorous to find a British outpost; to see British gunboats in the harbour and
hear cockney speech in the streets.

You may feel that you are nearer to Portsmouth
than Cathay, but when you climb the great hill

behind the town you get another impression. Westward beyond you in a mysterious golden haze are vistas into China, highlands and valleys, dim and inaccessible regions stretching away to the far mountain horizons.

There is the home of the vastest population of the earth, of the people of whom we know least, of the race which in proportion to its numbers has made less mark on the world than any other.

What happy chance, or what divine enlightenment is it that gives the secret of creative development to certain races,—that while "A Cycle of Cathay" and its innumerable people have hardly influenced the thought or aims of the modern world, so small a state as ancient Greece has been the purest source and remains the constant inspiration of its culture.

On our outward voyage in the sailing-ship we felt like explorers, and we were able to enter imaginatively into the life of the countries we visited: on our return journey we are but tourists. The comforts of a modern liner, our wireless communication with the London Stock Exchange, the cosmopolitan hotels at the ports of call, the world we bring with us,—all obscures our vision of the places we now approach.

284

India! We may land at Colombo and dine and dance at the Galle Face Hotel, perhaps visit Neuralia, perhaps endorse the unchristian words of a Christian Bishop:

> What though the spicy breezes
> Blow soft o'er Ceylon's isle,
> Where every prospect pleases
> And only man is vile.

Or we may have a few hours in the great city of Bombay, and remember some of the writing of the Englishman who was born there and who did more than any other man to interpret the life of India to his countrymen. Beyond lies a vast country, unlike China in that it is accessible and crossed by modern roads and railways, but having populations almost as alien in thought and tradition as China: a land which has a past in which magnificence and squalor, tyrannical power and servitude, existed side by side, whose teeming and partly educated masses are now awakening to a sense of the power which modern conditions have given to majorities. It is a land already overpopulated,—and where on the Earth shall room be found for its surplus? Again, dreaming of the future, we remember the limits of our island world and wonder what hope we may keep for the

285

survival of the noblest rather than of the most prolific.

And now we are approaching those countries of the earth whose histories open long vistas into the past, and whose fortunes and faiths have directed the destinies of the whole world. Picturing that visitor from another sphere in our company, wishing to interest him in our little world, how eager we should be to tell him of the wonder and romance that blossomed within those Arabian shores whose sandy promontories shimmer in the burning sunshine, to make him realise the enchantment of names like Baghdad and Samarcand and Harun-al-Rashid, and listen to the stories of magicians and genii, and peris.

And how could we adequately tell him, how would he receive that other story of the wise men who came from the East and the star shining over the manger in Bethlehem of Judea?

Can these lands we look out on from our ship be the same as those in which these scenes were enacted? Can that be the same Mount Sinai that Moses saw? We are bound to our own time and place, and are divided from the world of the past almost as widely as the earth we live on is separated from the other spheres.

OUR ISLAND WORLD

Our liner modelled on the latest plan
    Propels us down the coasts of Long-ago,—
    Our world with it: we hear the bugles blow
For meals, or under an electric fan
Doze or play bridge, or wireless head-lines scan,
    Or quoits of rope into a bucket throw.
    That was Mount Sinai in the sunset's glow,
And southward lay the land of Midian.
Night falls; above the water's undertone
    The band is heard, the decks are curtained in
    For dancing, and outbreaks a mingled din
Of talk and laughter, drum and saxophone.
Eastward across the sea, remote and lone,
    The moon rose o'er the Wilderness of Zin.

Entering the Mediterranean we are among
scenes which have been constantly present in our
imagination. The mystery and splendour of the
Orient is left behind, and a new atmosphere of
vitality, a deeper impression of beauty, have taken
their place. No seas on the earth are so enchanted
as those that wash the shores of Greece and Italy,
no events in the history of the world have been so
great as those which took place on the borders of
those seas; nor have natural beauty and lovely
legend ever been so happily combined as in those
waters,

287

A READING OF LIFE

Where every isle has a golden story,
And every haven a golden name.

We have been regretting that our earth is so
small, but its dimensions are measured for each
of us more truly by time than space, more in what
we can read than in what we can see. There was
a young man on our ship, a pleasant and healthy
young Englishman, whose outlook was an illustration of the limits to which the horizon of a life
may be narrowed. Unmoved by natural beauty or
historic interest, he dozed in a deck-chair through
the greater part of the days, from time to time
informing us that he was tired of this voyage,—
until we came to Port Said. Here he went ashore
and returned with eyes sparkling with animation,
to tell us that he had at last found something of
real interest. He had seen a hermaphrodite who
was on public view in that putrescent town. As
Goldsmith discovered,

Still to ourselves in every place consign'd
Our own felicity we make or find.

And now we are through the Straits of Gib-
raltar and out again on the great highway of the
world, the free waters that lead everywhere and
touch all shores,—the ocean, whose sound brings

tidings to all island wanderers of their native land. Finisterre is passed; and the grey-green seas of the Bay of Biscay that roll past us, the salt spray on our faces, and the exhilaration of our movement mingle with the expectancy of home-coming.

In a few hours we shall see across the waters the familiar landmarks of the shores we left, and in a few days, in our old homes again, look out on the horizons we saw in our childhood,—those hills beyond which lay the great world we pictured, a world larger and more wonderful than any we have been able to discover.

❋   ❋   ❋

In looking back on our voyage over the Earth our first reflection is that there are too many people on it already, and that a considerable proportion of its people does not belong to its best stock. It is true that there are parts of the Earth unsuited to be the dwelling-place of its best races, though habitable to inferior ones. Negroes may thrive in the swamps of West Africa, but they also thrive when trans-planted, and with a veneer of civilisation they have multiplied in the United States, and have there left the mark of the barbarian on the national being, into which has been embodied their corrupt speech, and the crude emotionalism of their music, dancing, and religion.

Millions of what seem to be ineffectual lives struggle for existence in China; and the European workman, who has the capacity and has won the right to a standard of living which allows reasonable comfort and leisure, has to compete economically with the factory hands of India and Japan, who accept and can live on a wage of less than a shilling a day.

Wars, famines, plagues kept down those Oriental populations in the past: modern conditions, scientific and mechanical progress, European intervention and rule, have done much to remove these restrictions, and it seems probable that their peoples will in the future form a still larger proportion of the world's population than at present.

As our hope for the future of our civilisation depends on the growth and predominant influence of our best stock, the new powers which modern conditions have given to numbers becomes a serious danger. Unless some great counteracting movement, some revolt against the present tendencies of development, surprises the world, the inferior races and the inferior classes of the superior races will occupy a place on the earth out of all proportion to the contribution they make to its progress.

There never was a time when it was so important for the leaders of those nations which have traditions and ideals to keep their highest standards in front of their own peoples, and to make these ideals a bond of cosmopolitan union. A League of Nations thus united could take responsibility for the guidance of the world. While cherishing everything that is worthiest of their national pride, they may join forces in the promotion of a terrestrial pride.

No forecasts of the future have ever been correct: they invariably project the tendencies of the present, and these are almost always deflected by unforeseen events. Our hope must be that the forecasts at present being made by our prophets, of a world dominated by mechanical development, a world whose highways have been removed to the skies, whose buildings out-scrape the sky-scrapers of New York, whose speed of transport is almost incredible, whose lethal weapons could at any time let loose Hell upon Earth, may be falsified by some new and unexpected event in the spiritual evolution of man, some deeper understanding of the things that make life really worth living, some new inspiration that will redirect his energies.

The change which mechanical development has made on the Earth's surface has begun to awaken man to a sense of his responsibility for the preservation of its beauty. Until the last hundred years his invasion of Nature's sanctuaries, his settlement in new regions, were done naturally, and when the beauty of the wild was injured it was replaced by a beauty of habitation. Even during the last hundred years he needed little excuse for his desecration of lovely places by railways, factories, mines, and other developments which offered relief to populations confronted with poverty or even starvation; but now that the prospect of a starving world is so far removed that superfluous stores of wheat, coffee, and other products of the soil have actually been destroyed to keep up their market prices, the excuse of necessity no longer exists. No one who can remember England fifty years ago, and sees to-day its exquisite villages mutilated by motor tracks, its lovely sea-board vulgarised by garish watering-places, can contemplate without anger the lack of national pride in a great inheritance that can permit a licence for spoilation in the interest of unnecessary utilitarian expedients or of commercial acquisitiveness.

It is difficult to turn back: mechanical and chemical developments cannot be stopped, but they must be guided, governed by man's wisdom, or their soulless dominion will ruin the world. Some feeble attempts are being made to prevent the high-roads from being converted by motor traffic into scenes of slaughter; and the effort to limit the infernal efficiency of the engines of war by international agreement is a step towards sanity. The machine is a boon to both fool and knave. A man of little worth, but with enough intelligence to control a bit of mechanism,—a rogue with a revolver, a cad with a motor car,—is given a power to which he has no right. How often have we seen this in the drivers of huge motor vehicles who dominate a road and convert the momentum of the machine into human brutality. We must hope that man will have learned the lesson of present tendencies in time to prevent the frustration of civilised ideals in a war of chemical murder or a peace of mechanised enslavement.

How proud man ought to feel in having the care of so beautiful a sphere, so loveable a home as the Earth. He might have been born on a planet

where he would have had scant reward for his
labours,—a world of arctic regions or torrid
swamps, a world through whose cloudy canopy he
would have had no view of the heavens, or one
where volcano and earthquake kept him in constant terror. But on Earth he finds physical conditions which he could hardly improve on in his
rosiest dreams. The axis of the Earth is set at an
angle which ensures variety of temperature and a
succession of seasons favourable to his activities,
the ocean which separates its lands is a safeguard
of perennial purification, and the soil of the Earth
itself forbids corruption. "Earth makes all sweet"
as Meredith says.

Contemplating these wonders, and all the
Earth's lovely scenes of mountain and moorland,
rivers and sea-shores, what would our imagined
visitor think of man's trusteeship when he beheld
rivers polluted with drainage and factory effluents,
oil discharged from ships that fouled the surface
of the waters and killed the sea birds, shapeless
distensions and deformed tentacles of modern
towns that enwrap the countryside? A depressing
spectacle! But side by side with this failure he
would see evidences of the fidelity of man's
stewardship and the nobility of his labours. Be-

holding in man the dominant creature on Earth, who has invented poison gas for the destruction of his fellow creatures, but in the depths of whose spirit is mercy and loving-kindness,—who has mutilated the beauty of the earth by his greed and stupidity, but has lifted the soaring spires from the quarry and drawn heavenly music from a string, well might he depart

> Twi-minded of him as the waxing tree
> Or dated leaf.

Now that there are no new lands or seas to discover, much of the mystery has been taken from our island world; but the mystery of the unknown, the call of adventure, remains; and as the limitations of the earth deny further exploration to man, he will find new pathways of adventure and discovery within his own spirit,—pathways that in time may prove a bond of communication between his mortal life and an eternal purpose. We often complain that we are born into a universe which we cannot comprehend, but if we had been shown nothing except that which was obvious or explainable, the spirit would have had no outlet for expansion, no pathway to wonderland. Man's spirit, I believe, responds to the influence of eternal truth: in his pursuit of truth much that was mysterious has grown clear, but he has learned that his discoveries are always on the borderland of new mysteries.

Having now explored and charted our island world, we know that adventure is at an end until the spirit can create its exodus; but we may also rejoice in the compensations that have been given to us in the confines and isolation of our abode. In that incomprehensible, untraversable scene of the life of which we are part, the boundaries of the Earth have made us a home and given us shelter in the vast. Glad to forget the immeasurability and incomprehensible wonder of celestial pathways whose milestones are light-years, we bless the field-paths and lanes of the little Earth on which we have met as comrades or kept our trysts as lovers.

All those who have found the companions whose love has filled their hearts can feel that the earth has given them, in what its narrow boundaries have brought together, gifts that they would not exchange for the promise of a freedom which those boundaries have denied.

Man is earth's child and its ruler,—the recipient of its vital forces and also their treasurer. There are times when calm reason tells him that his own life must share the mortality of the Earth which produced it, that his spirit is a flash of light that must be extinguished when the structure through which it shone is in ashes. And there are moments of illumination in which he feels that his lineage is older than the Earth's, and his spirit greater than its embodiment; when instead of concluding that every ideal, every purpose, every inspiration of the life he has held will ultimately perish with the Earth's fabric, he can believe that all the good things the Earth has shown him, all things that inspired his devotion, have an eternal significance, and abide in the treasury of a Divine Spirit of which human love is a part.

THE END